THE
HOT AND
·SPICY·
COOKBOOK

SOPHIE HALE

THE
HOT AND
·SPICY·
COOKBOOK

SOPHIE HALE

Grange
BOOKS

A QUINTET BOOK

This edition published 1993 by Grange Books
An imprint of Grange Books Plc
The Grange, Grange Yard, London SE1 3AG

ISBN 1-85627-482-9

Reprinted 1994

This book was designed and produced by
Quintet Publishing Limited
6 Blundell Street
London N7 9BH

Art Director: Peter Bridgewater
Editors: Fanny Campbell, Josephine Bacon
Photographer: Trevor Wood
Food Preparation and Styling: Jonathan R.
Higgins
Illustrator: Lorraine Harrison

Typeset in Great Britain by
Central Southern Typesetters, Eastbourne
Manufactured in Hong Kong by
Regent Publishing Services Limited
Printed in Singapore by
Star Standard Industries Pte Ltd

The author and publishers would like to thank
House Food Industrial Company (Japan) for
permission to reproduce the illustratrions on
pages 10 and 11.

✦ CONTENTS ✦

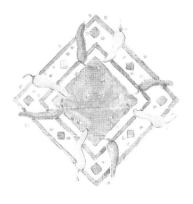

◆ INTRODUCTION ◆

SPICE may be the variety of life, but hot and spicy goes one better. Food that is both hot and spicy combines flavour with sensation to enhance the bland, disguise the questionable, and appeal to mankind's age-old passion for novelty by making food that much more exciting. The countless ways in which seasonings are used are what gives each of the world's great cuisines its unique savour, from the curries, satays and sambals of the mystic East to the chilli (chili) of the Wild West, uniting the Old World with the New.

The spice trade is probably the oldest of all; expeditions are recorded from Egypt to the east coast of Africa some 4,000 years ago. The spice trade was — and still is — among the most lucrative, and, despite the enormous and mostly uncharted distances and financial and personal risks involved, attracted successfully the Phoenicians, Romans, Arabs, Venetians, Genoese, Spanish, Portuguese, Dutch, British and Americans.

Peppercorns, mustard and Chinese ginger were the source of culinary heat until Columbus changed the course of hot and spicy history by taking an Atlantic route to spice-rich India and discovering the Americas — and chillies (chilies) — instead. The European explorers and traders planted these spices wherever their tropical and subtropical travels took them, including the West Indies, Indonesia and, of course, India . . .

Variety is the life of spice, especially in the kitchen, so why not experiment, using this book to guide you through the hot and spicy spectrum, from subtle to fiery, soup to nuts. Whatever you do, it certainly won't be boring!

◆ SPICE LIST ◆

ALLSPICE, so named because its flavour is said to combine those of cloves, nutmeg, cinnamon and pepper, is the reddish brown dried berry of *Pimenta officinalis,* an evergreen related to the myrtle. It is also known as "pimento", because the first European to encounter it, in Mexico, took it to be some kind of pepper, and "Jamaica pepper" after its other main habitat. Allspice is versatile to cook with, enhancing both sweet and savoury dishes. Traditionally used in the pickling spice mixture for herrings, beef and vegetables, and in Christmas puddings, pork sausages and sweet mince pies, it is also good in fruit salads, especially pineapple, baked bananas, rum punch and even with spinach.

ANISEED, also called "anise", is the dried and sometimes roasted seed of *Pimpinella anisum,* a feathery plant related to fennel, originally from the Middle East. Its distinctive flavour is probably best known

through liqueurs like pernod, ouzo and arak and aniseed-flavoured candy. Used in small quantities, aniseed is good in fish soups and curries and, following the example of the Romans who used them as a digestive, spicy little cakes and cookies. "Star anise", that vital component of so much of Chinese cuisine, has a similar flavour, but is not related; it is the seed of *Illicum verum,* a kind of southeast Asian magnolia. Combined with equal quantities of fennel seed, cassia, cloves and Szechuan pepper it is a component of the Chinese five-spice powder.

CARAWAY, the seeds of *Carum cervi,* has been known for at least 5,000 years as a flavouring, a digestive and as a protection against the evil eye. It is native to both western Asia and Europe, especially Germany, where it is used to flavour liqueurs like kümmel and in stews and dumplings. Often an ingredient in curry powders and pastes (see recipe), caraway is also good in cheese dishes and breads, with potatoes, cabbage and baked apples and in seed cake, a great favourite of Victorian tea parties.

CARDAMOM, the tiny, black and intensely fragrant seeds of *Ellataria cardamomum,* a herb related to ginger (see below), is an essential ingredient in much Indian, southeast Asian, Middle Eastern and North African cooking, as well as in many European cakes and desserts; the whole pods are often served as a postprandial palate restorer. Use them in their pods, lightly bruised, in rice dishes, apple strudel and mulled wine, crush them for curries and cookies, or sprinkle them on after-dinner coffee or tea. Cardamom is, after saffron and cloves (see below) the most expensive of spices to buy.

CAYENNE pepper is the finely ground seeds and pods of *Capsicum frutescens* and *Capsicum minimum,* members of the plant family that includes chillies (chilies) (see below). It is traditionally used to season

cheese dishes, fish soups and patés, and in devilled dishes and barbecues. As it is so strong, a pinch or two is usually enough.

CHILLIES (chilies) cover a variety of small, hot, brilliantly-coloured capsicums, and, according to evidence found in 9,000-year-old Mexican and Peruvian burial sites, were probably the earliest flavouring to be cultivated. The capsicum family, named after the latin for "container", also includes the sweet, or bell, pepper *(Capsicum annuum)* so good in salads. The hot varieties are grown for cayenne pepper and Tabasco sauce, and the milder for paprika (see below). Although they are all known as "peppers", they are in no way related to black pepper, *Piper nigrum* (see Peppercorns).

Nowadays they are widely grown in almost all tropical and subtropical countries, generally starting green and ripening to a bright red which is usually hotter and has more flavour. The actual strength varies from type to type; the Jamaican Scotch Bonnet, Mexican *chile pequin* and the Japanese Hontaka are among the hottest. Dried chillies (chilies) are widely available; they need soaking in hot water for 20 minutes to half an hour before use). Canned chillies (chilies) particularly the versatile Mexican jalapeño, are also much used in cooking.

Commercially-produced chilli (chili) powder often includes other flavourings, such as cumin, garlic salt and oregano; if you want to be sure of what you're getting, buy dried chillies (chilies) and grind them yourself. The strength of chilli (chili) powders can vary from brand to brand, so be cautious; heat is always easier to add than subtract. The recipes in this book are for hot chilli (chili) powder; and you should assume that any you buy *will* be hot, unless labelled to the contrary.

The world's greatest cuisines have evolved their own, enormously varied ways of using chillies (chilies), from Mexico's ceremonial Mole Poblano with its unique chocolate and chilli (chili) sauce made with the dark-brown *chile poblano*, to the delicate curries of Kashmir, rich in cream and almonds, from classic Texan "bowl of red" chili con carne, the end of every cowboy's weary trail, to satay, fragrant, hot and slightly sweet, the flavour of southeast Asia.

CINNAMON is the inner bark of a kind of Asiatic laurel, *Cinnamomum zeylanicum*, rolled into quills and dried. The Chinese have been using it since 2,500 BC, while according to Exodus (xxx:23) its oil was among those with which Moses

was to anoint the tabernacle. As readyground cinnamon loses its aroma so quickly, it is better to buy it in quill (stick) form. The quills can be ground or crushed for use in all manner of cakes, pastries and milder curries, stewed fruit, custards, rice pudding, chocolate mousse and, whole, in mulled wine. "Cassia", also known as "Chinese cinnamon", is the thicker, slightly cruder flavoured bark of the *Cinnamomum cassia* tree, a close relative of cinnamon with an equally long history. Ground cassia is often sold as cinnamon, especially in spice mixtures for baking.

CLOVES, from the Latin for "nail", are the dried, unopened flower buds of *Syzygium aromaticum,* an evergreen tree originating in the Moluccas, Indonesia's Spice Islands, and now flourishing along Africa's tropical coast, particularly in Zanzibar. The most pungently aromatic of all spices, the oil is used in perfumery and medicinally as a local anaesthetic for toothaches. Try studding boiled and sugared hams with whole cloves before baking, and they are a good flavouring for bread sauce (see recipe), rice, stews, apple pies and mulled wine. A pinch or so of ground cloves goes well in the milder curries, sweet buns and cheesecakes.

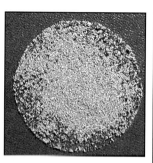

CORIANDER is the small yellowish-brown seed of *Coriandrum sativum*, and has been known in the East for thousands of years, where it is an important ingredient in Garam Masala (see recipe) and curry flavourings, and is also grown in North Africa, Mexico and southern Europe. Freshly crushed, coriander seeds have a faintly orangey tang that adds a delicately exotic breath to a wide range of sweet and savoury dishes including roast chicken (see recipe), dal (see recipe) kebabs and sweet spice mixes (see recipe). The leaves, also known in the English speaking world as Chinese parsley and cilantro, are strongly aromatic, and are popular in Greek, Mexican and Indian cookery.

CUMIN, *Cuminum cyminum,* originated in the East where the warm, spicy smell of its seeds, both whole and ground, permeate most aspects of the various cuisines, particularly curries. It has been grown in Mediterranean countries for some 2,000 years, and is

now one of the most widely cultivated spices of all. The seeds are similar in appearance to those of caraway and aniseed, but the fragrance is unique, enhancing chicken, fish, rice and lamb dishes, cabbage, chilli (chili), many European breads, cheeses and liqueurs, and homemade sausages.

FENUGREEK, *Trigonella foenum-graecum,* also known as "Greek hay", is what gives most curry powders their pungency. A member of the pea family, it originated in Asia but is now grown in India, North Africa, western Asia and parts of Europe. The seeds are yellowish-brown, very hard, and have to be heated to release their smell. They act as a thickener as well as a slightly bitter flavouring. They are also highly nutritious. Fenugreek has been used as an animal feed, and even as a hair restorer. They are particularly good in vegetable curries, onion bhajis (see recipe) and, sprouted, as a salad ingredient.

GINGER is the rhizome (underground root) of *Zingiber officinale* and over the past 2,500 years has come to stand for all that is hot and spicy. It originated in India and China — the Chinese version being the hotter-tasting — and was well-known in Europe by the 11th century. It was brought to the New World in the 16th century. Fresh, or "green", it looks like a Jerusalem artichoke and, peeled and grated, pounded or finely chopped, is a feature of many Indian, southeast Asian and Chinese meat and fish dishes and an interesting addition to both green and fruit salads, while dried and ground — the palest and most delicately flavoured comes from Jamaica — it is used in all manner of cakes, biscuits (cookies) and fruit puddings. Crystallized (candied) ginger or stem ginger preserved in syrup are popular sweatmeats and are good chopped into ice creams, syllabubs and fruitcakes.

MACE is the lacy scarlet covering around the nutmeg seed (see below). Its flavour, though similar, is slightly more refined and is traditionally associated with fish and shellfish, especially potted shrimps. It is also very good in spiced beef, braised pork and chicken, and in spice cake. You can take it off whole nutmegs and break it gently into small pieces as needed, or buy it readyground.

MUSTARD seeds, ground and mixed to a paste with flavoured vinegar or wine, has proved a popular condiment since Roman times. The name derives from "must" or new wine and "ardens", latin for "burning". Mustard will flourish in most temperate climates, making it the most widely available of spices. There are at least three varieties, but only two are used commercially: brown mustard, *Brassica juncea,* and white, *Sinapis alba.* The French and most other Europeans prefer the former, while English mustard is made from a combination. Whole mustard seeds are used in pickling spice and curry powders, and the condiment is good in cheese sauces, devilled dishes, in dressings for salads and cooked vegetables, and with roast beef and sausages.

NUTMEG, the inner kernel of the nut of the *Myristica fragrans,* has long been popular in European kitchens. It originated in the Moluccas, the East Indies, and was introduced into Penang and the West Indies by the British in the early 19th century. Nutmeg can be used in curries, béchamel and cheese sauces, fruit cakes and sweet and savoury soufflés and is an esssential flavouring in baked bananas (see recipe), rum punch and mulled wine. Nutmeg can be bought ready-ground but, as with so many spices, it quickly loses its aroma; it is far better to get whole nutmegs in their hard outer casing (with the mace (see above) still on if you're lucky) and grate it as needed.

PAPRIKA is the dried and ground flesh of sweet red pepper, *Capsicum annuum.* It is popular all over Europe, particularly in Hungary, where the best paprika is produced. It is an essential ingredient in veal goulash, but paprika's rich red colour and mildly spicy taste is also good in tomato sauces, stews and chilli (chili), and to cheer up pallid-looking pastry, sauces and gratins.

PEPPERCORNS, *Piper nigrum,* are the most commonly used spice of all, as well as one of the oldest. They are the dried berries of a vine native to India's Malabar coast, but which also grows in Indonesia, Thailand, equatorial Africa and the South Sea Islands. Black and white peppercorns are essentially the same, the stronger white pepper being the berry with its aromatic coating removed before drying, while green peppercorns are the unripe green berries pickled in brine and canned or bottled. Before chillies (chilies) (see above) were introduced into the Indian sub-continent and southeast Asia from Mexico, curries relied on peppercorns for their heat. Ground pepper loses its flavour fast, so always use freshly-ground pepper, black or white — the latter in pale sauces and fish dishes — for both cooking and eating. A combination of black and white corns in your pepper mill is known as mignonette pepper, and makes a pleasant mixture, as does the addition of a few whole allspice.

POPPYSEEDS are used for flavouring many European breads and pastries and for seasoning and thickening curries. They come from several varieties of the flower, including *Papaver somniferum,* the opium poppy, the seeds of which are not narcotic. Poppyseeds range in colour from blue-black to almost white. They are very hard and need grinding if used in cakes and curries, though they are sprinkled whole on breads. They can be ground in a coffee grinder.

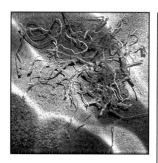
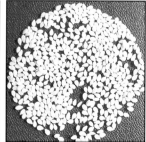
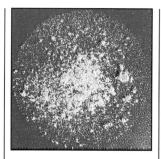

SAFFRON, the dried stigmas of the saffron crocus, *Crocus sativa* is the most highly prized of spices, its heady scent and glorious orangey-gold colour has long been associated with royalty. As the stigmas of some 75,000 crocuses are needed to produce 450 g/1 lb of the spice, saffron is also the most expensive of spices. Native to the Mediterranean as well as Asia Minor, Kashmir and Iran, saffron is a feature of fish dishes like bouillabaisse, paella and the milk sauce and pilafs. It is important to buy saffron in its thread form — it will need to be infused in hot water before using; substances sold as ground saffron are pretty sure to be turmeric (see below).

RIGHT: *Ginger roots being sorted for purchase.*

SESAME SEEDS, from the *Sesamum indicum,* have a deliciously nutty flavour and can be sprinkled on breads and cakes, Chinese candied apples or bananas, curries, and gratins of fish, eggs or vegetables for a crunchy topping. Ground, they feature in *halva, tahini* dip and *tarator* sauce, while the oil is used in salads and to finish many Chinese dishes. The plant is probably of Middle Eastern origin, but is now cultivated in most subtropical areas, including India, Thailand and the Americas.

TURMERIC is the boiled, dried and ground rhizome of *Curcuma longa,* a plant related to ginger (see above) and native to southern India and Indonesia. Its yellow colour and mildly bitter flavour contribute to most curry powders and flavourings, and are good in onion sauce, leek gratin and smoked fish dishes. Like saffron, turmeric is used as a dye and a cosmetic in parts of Asia and it can be substituted for saffron (see above) to colour rice yellow, though a difference in flavour will probably be noticed.

VANILLA, the cured and dried bean pods of the climbing orchid *Vanilla planifolia,* was originally used by the Aztecs to flavour their chocolate drink, *choclatl,* though it is now grown throughout the tropics and is a universal flavouring ingredient in sweet dishes. To release the flavour, either infuse the bean in hot liquid, as for Vanilla Brûlée (see recipe) or use vanilla sugar — white sugar stored in an airtight container with a well-bruised vanilla pod. You can also use vanilla essence (extract), although the flavour isn't as good. Vanilla is so popular that a chemical flavouring has been created to imitate it, and it is this chemical that is used in products marked "vanilla-flavoured".

OPPOSITE: *Spices and vegetables on sale in a market.*

Hot and spicy cookery isn't quite so simple as it sounds. Anyone can chuck in the chilli (chili) powder and hope for the best, but it is more than likely to cauterize your taste buds and drive you hot-throat to the nearest beer or handy horse-trough; in any case, flavourings used indiscriminately simply cancel each other out. But chilli (chili) and its variants, judiciously combined with complementary spices, can be orchestrated into an infinite range of flavours, sensations and aromas: savoury or sweet; subtle or fiery; simple or multi-layered; a saxophone solo or the Hallelujah Chorus. Still, we all know of times when that four-alarm curry or blistering bowl of chilli con carne is the only thing that will hit the spot. Whatever you do, and the scope for experiment is bounded only by your imagination, it is worth bearing the following in mind:

"Heat" tolerance varies from person to person: one man's mildly spicy can be another's four-alarm fire. So, if you are in any doubt concerning the mettle of your guests — or your own — reduce the quantity of chillies (chilies) or chilli (chili) powder, or, if using the latter, substitute the mild variety. The chilli (chili) powder used in these recipes is *hot*, as will be any you buy, unless specified otherwise. You can always zap it up later with a few drops of Pepper Wine (see recipe), Tabasco, or other commercially-produced hot pepper sauce. If, however, your dish is *too* hot, do not add sugar, but substitute coconut water or coconut milk (see Malaysian Fish Curry) for the remaining liquid. If no more liquid is needed, add yogurt, or ground poppyseeds and a little lemon juice.

Always wash your hands well after preparing fresh chillies (chilies), or wear rubber gloves. Avoid getting the juice near your eyes or lips; this can be very painful, and takes a long time to wear off. The seeds are the hottest part, so make sure you have scraped or picked out every one. When directed to grill (broil) chillies (chilies) until their skins "blister" (as for

Chillies In Oil), watch them carefully, but be careful how closely you watch them; the acridly pungent fumes of burning chilli (chili) were a popular torture method.

Buying spices, either at your local health food shop, speciality store or ethnic supermarket, do not get more than 25 g/1 oz or so at a time, especially if they are ready-ground. Grind them yourself if possible, preferably just before use. To do this, warm them through first in a moderate oven to release their fragrance, then use a coffee grinder, ideally one reserved for the purpose. For really small quantities, a pepper mill is just the thing. Once ground, they should be kept in light-proof, airtight containers and stored in a cool, dry place. Even so, ground spices will begin to lose their aroma in about 3 weeks, and should be replaced as soon as they begin to smell "musty".

Try not to have more than one particularly hot and/or spicy dish per meal. Contrasting strengths of flavour and serving temperatures also complement each other; so serve a strong curry with plenty of plain boiled rice or Nan (Indian bread, see recipe) and a cooling salad, accompanied perhaps by chilled slices of fresh fruit — such as mango and nectarine — and a bowl of cold minted, yogurt or sour cream; a highly-flavoured vegetable, salad, sauce, dressing or relish is excellent with a mild-tasting main course or cold meat. Vary intensity of flavour from course to course: a strong main dish either preceded by a "fiery" starter or followed by a rich, highly-spiced dessert can be tough on the digestion.

Although cold beer and soft drinks are consumed in large quantities with "hot" foods, alcoholic drinks have the effect of exaggerating the heat. Milk, coconut water or yogurt drink (plain yogurt thinned with a little ice water) are far more thirst quenching.

Even if your meal is not so highly-flavoured, it isn't worth drinking the best wine. Instead, try spritz (dry white wine and soda water) or a red or white *vin ordinaire* or *vin de table*.

◆ Snacks ◆

◆ PPC FINGERS ◆

MAKES APPROX. 35

2 pitta (pita) breads

40 g/1½ oz Parmesan cheese, freshly grated is nicest

Pinch of cayenne

Approx. 2 tbsp/25 g/1 oz butter, softened

Extra cayenne (optional)

◆ Grill (broil) the pittas (pitas) on both sides until lightly browned, and split them while still warm.

◆ Mix the Parmesan and cayenne. Spread the un-toasted pitta (pita) sides with the butter and sprinkle evenly with the cheese mixture.

◆ Cut into fingers 2.5 cm (1 in) wide, arrange on a baking tray (cookie sheet) and grill (broil) at a high heat until the cheese begins to brown and bubble.

◆ Serve warm, dusted with extra cayenne if you like.

A crunchy combination of Parmesan, pitta (pita) and cayenne, ideal for pre-dinner drinks.

◆ CHEESE AND MUSTARD STRAWS ◆

MAKES APPROX. 50

1½ cups/150 g/6 oz plain (all-purpose) flour

Good pinch salt

Good pinch white pepper

2.5 g/½ tsp ground turmeric

½ cup/100 g/4 oz butter, softened

10 g/2 tsp English mustard OR 15 g/1 tbsp coarse-grained French mustard

30 g/2 tbsp Parmesan cheese, freshly grated if possible

1 egg yolk

Ice water

OVEN TEMPERATURE: 200°C/400°F/GAS 6

◆ Sift together the flour, salt, white pepper and turmeric. Rub in the butter and mustard until the mixture resembles fine crumbs.

◆ Stir in the Parmesan cheese, egg yolk and just enough ice water to hold the dough together.

◆ Roll out to about 6 mm (¼ in) thick and slice into straws about 10 cm (4 in) long, and 6 mm (¼ in) wide.

◆ Arrange them, a little apart from each other, on greased baking trays (cookie sheets) and bake in a preheated oven until crisp and golden, about 7 minutes. Serve warm.

◆ These can be baked in advance and reheated, and also freeze well.

VARIATION The straws can also be cut into 3 cm (1½ in) rounds.

✦ DEVILLED NUTS ✦

INGREDIENTS

MAKES 225 G/8 OZ

225 g/8 oz shelled nuts (almonds, peanuts, cashews or a mixture)

15 ml/1 tbsp oil

1 tbsp/15 g/½ oz butter

1 clove garlic, crushed (minced)

Rock salt

Cayenne

PREPARATION

◆ Pour boiling water over the almonds, refresh in cold water and slip off the skins. Toast the peanuts for 2 minutes and rub off the skins in a tea (dish) towel.

◆ Heat the oil and butter in a heavy frying pan (skillet) and fry the garlic for a few seconds.

◆ Add the nuts, reduce the heat to moderate and toss the nuts until crisp and golden, 4 to 6 minutes.

◆ Drain on kitchen paper (paper towels) and toss in rock salt and cayenne. Serve warm.

VARIATION For Bombay Beans, substitute canned chick peas (garbanzos), well drained and patted dry, for the nuts.

◆ ONION BHAJIS ◆

MAKES 10–12
30 ml/2 tbsp oil
2.5 g/½ tsp ground mustard seed
5 g/1 tsp fenugreek seed
5 g/1 tsp ground turmeric
1 medium onion, finely chopped
Pinch chilli (chili) powder (optional)
2.5 g/½ tsp salt
1 egg
1 cup/100 g/4 oz gram (chick pea) flour
Oil for frying

PREPARATION

◆ Heat the oil and fry the spices for a minute. Add the onion, and stir until well coated.

◆ Turn down the heat, cover, and cook until the onion is tender but not mushy. Leave to cool.

◆ Add salt, egg and gram (chick pea) flour and stir well.

◆ Fry generous half-tablespoonfuls of the mixture in 1 cm (½ in) hot oil, turning them almost immediately. As soon as they are puffy and brown remove them with a slotted spoon and drain on kitchen paper (paper towels). Serve warm.

◆ Onion Bhajis can be kept warm in a moderate oven for 20 minutes or so before serving, but they cannot be made in advance and reheated.

VARIATION Make the bhajis half-size and serve with toothpicks or cocktail sticks.

◆ FISH KOFTA ◆

INGREDIENTS

SERVES 4 – 6

350 g/12 oz cooked firm white fish

1 small onion, grated

5 g/1 tsp ground coriander

2.5 g/½ tsp ground turmeric

2.5 g/½ tsp ground cumin

2.5 g/½ tsp chilli (chili) powder

Pinch ground ginger

15 ml/1 tbsp lime juice

Salt to taste

2 eggs, lightly beaten

Breadcrumbs

Oil for frying

PREPARATION

◆ Mash or process together all the ingredients except the eggs, breadcrumbs and oil

◆ Form into small balls, roll in the beaten egg and then in the breadcrumbs, and deep or shallow fry until golden.

◆ Drain on kitchen paper (paper towels) and serve hot, with toothpicks or cocktail sticks and perhaps a choice of dips.

◆ NACHOS ◆

INGREDIENTS

MAKES 32 PIECES

1 small onion or 3 spring (green) onions, finely chopped

2 fresh green chillies (chilies), seeded and finely chopped

Approx. 45 ml/3 tbsp oil

8 bought corn tortillas or Flour Tortillas (see recipe)

75 g/3 oz strong Cheddar cheese, shredded or grated

PREPARATION

➤ Fry the onion or spring (green) onions with the chillies (chilies) in a little of the oil until softened and beginning to brown. Drain and reserve.

➤ Add the rest of the oil to the pan and fry the tortillas on both sides until golden. Drain each on kitchen paper (paper towels) and keep warm while you fry the rest.

➤ Arrange the fried tortillas on a baking tray (cookie sheet), sprinkle with the onion and chilli mixture and top with grated cheese.

➤ Grill (broil) under a high heat until the cheese melts.

➤ Stack the Nachos, quarter them and serve immediately.

NOTE If made in advance, the cold, fried tortillas and their topping can be baked at a preheated 220°C/425°F/Gas 7 for 5 to 7 minutes, so that the tortilla bases are well heated through.

◆ SOUPS & STARTERS ◆

◆ CHILLED TOMATO CHILLI (CHILI) SOUP ◆

INGREDIENTS

SERVES 4

2 large tomatoes, skinned, seeded and quartered

2 spring (green) onions, chopped

5 g/1 tsp chilli (chili) powder

2.5 g/½ tsp ground coriander

5 g/1 tsp sugar

15 ml/1 tbsp lemon juice

Salt and freshly ground black pepper

Ice cubes

Chopped chives

PREPARATION

◆ Liquidize or process together until smooth everything except the ice cubes and chives. Chill.

◆ Correct the seasoning and serve cold, with an ice cube or two in each bowl and a sprinkling of chopped chives. A dollop of thick sour cream or crème fraîche is a good addition.

◆ SAFFRON FISH SOUP WITH ROUILLE ◆

INGREDIENTS

SERVES 6

1 large onion, chopped

3 cloves garlic, crushed (minced)

75 ml/5 tbsp olive oil

30 g/2 tbsp tomato purée (paste)

1.35 kg/3 lb fish and fish trimmings, cut into 5 cm (2 in) chunks

1½ quarts/1.5 l/2½ pt water

1¼ cups/300 ml/½ pt dry white wine

Bayleaf

A few sprigs thyme

2.5 g/½ tsp saffron threads, more if you're feeling generous

2.5 g/½ tsp sugar

Salt and freshly ground black pepper

450 g/1 lb potatoes, peeled and cut into 2.5 cm (1 in) chunks

12 slices crisply toasted French bread

Grated Parmesan cheese (freshly grated, if possible)

ROUILLE

1-2 fresh red chillies (chilies), split and seeded

1 canned pimiento (sweet red pepper), chopped

3-4 cloves garlic, finely crushed (minced)

60 ml/4 tbsp olive oil

Salt to taste

PREPARATION

◆ Soften the onion and garlic in the oil over a gentle heat, then add the tomato purée (paste) and cook for a few minutes more.

◆ Add the fish and fish trimmings, water, wine, herbs, saffron, sugar and seasoning, bring to the boil and simmer, uncovered, for half an hour.

◆ Strain the liquid into another pan, add the potatoes and simmer until tender, 15 to 20 minutes. Scoop out a quarter of the potatoes with a slotted spoon, and reserve.

◆ Sieve, liquidize or process the soup: it should not be too smooth. Return to the pan and correct seasoning.

◆ To make the Rouille, first simmer the chilli(es) (chili(es)) in a little salted water until tender. Rinse and chop finely.

◆ Pound, liquidize or process the chilli, pimiento (sweet red pepper), garlic and reserved potato to a thick, smooth paste, then add the oil, a little at a time, as if making mayonnaise. Season to taste.

◆ To serve, reheat the soup and gradually add a couple of tablespoonfuls of it to the sauce.

◆ Put 2 slices of toasted French bread into each bowl, pour over the soup, and pass the Rouille and Parmesan separately.

This aromatic relative of bouillabaisse is served with a marvellously hot and garlicky sauce. Almost any kind of lean fish can be used, with an equal quantity of fish trimmings.

◆ CORN AND CHILLI CHOWDER ◆

INGREDIENTS

SERVES 3—4

1-2 fresh red chillies (chilies)

1 medium onion, finely chopped

3 tbsp/40 g/1½ oz butter

1½ cups/225 g/8 oz canned or frozen sweetcorn kernels

2½ cups/600 ml/1 pt milk

Salt and pepper to taste

½ sweet red pepper, cored, seeded and thinly sliced or finely diced (optional)

PREPARATION

◆ Split and seed the chillies (chilies) and soak them in cold salted water for an hour, changing the water occasionally. Rinse and chop finely.

◆ Soften the chillies (chilies) and the onion in the butter, then add the sweetcorn and cook for a minute more, stirring well.

◆ Add the milk, cover, and simmer for 7 minutes.

◆ Sieve, liquidize or process all, or only half of the soup. It should not be too smooth.

◆ Reheat, season and serve, garnished, if you like, with sweet pepper.

◆ CURRIED PARSNIP SOUP ◆

INGREDIENTS

SERVES 3–4

Generous 450 g/1 lb parsnips

4 tbsp/50 g/2 oz butter

7.5 g/1½ tsp ground coriander

5 g/1 tsp ground cumin

2.5 g/½ tsp ground turmeric

Approx. 2½ cups/600 ml/1 pt milk and stock or water, mixed

Few drops Tabasco

Salt and white pepper to taste

30 ml/2 tbsp single (light) cream

Chopped fresh coriander or parsley

PREPARATION

◆ Scrub and trim the parsnips and chop into 2 cm (¾ in) dice. Cover with cold water until needed.

◆ Melt the butter in a heavy saucepan and fry the spices in it without browning to release the flavours.

◆ Add the drained parsnips and turn until well coated. Add the milk and stock or water and simmer, covered, for 20 minutes or so, until the parsnips are just tender.

◆ Sieve, liquidize or process the soup: it should not be absolutely smooth.

◆ Reheat and season to taste with Tabasco, salt and white pepper.

◆ Serve with a swirl of cream in each bowl, together with a sprinkling of fresh coriander or parsley.

◆ Curried Croûtons (see Curry Butter) are also good with this.

WARM GREEN (STRING OR SNAP) BEANS
WITH MUSTARD VINAIGRETTE

INGREDIENTS

SERVES 4

1 clove garlic, crushed (minced)

2.5 g/½ tsp sugar

15 g/1 tbsp mild Dijon-style mustard

15 ml/1 tbsp tarragon vinegar

60 ml/4 tbsp good olive oil

550 g/1¼ lb fresh young green (string or snap) beans, topped, tailed (trimmed) and stringed if necessary

Freshly ground black pepper

Yolks of 2-3 hard-boiled (hard-cooked) eggs

PREPARATION

◆ Mix the garlic, sugar and mustard together and add the vinegar and oil.

◆ Cook the green (string or snap) beans in lots of boiling salted water until just tender, 5 to 7 minutes.

◆ Drain in a colander and run hot water over them briefly.

◆ Pour the dressing over the beans and toss gently. Season with plenty of black pepper and transfer to a serving dish.

◆ Serve warm, sprinkled with chopped egg yolk.

Guacomole

◆ GUACAMOLE ◆

INGREDIENTS

SERVES 4

2 ripe avocado pears

1 small onion, roughly chopped or grated

1 tomato, peeled, seeded and finely chopped

1 clove garlic, crushed (minced)

½-1½ fresh green chillies (chilies), seeded and chopped

15 ml/1 tbsp lime or lemon juice

Good pinch salt

PREPARATION

◆ Halve the avocados and scoop out the flesh. Combine in a mortar, blender or food processor with the rest of the ingredients and reduce to a smooth purée, adding a little water if the mixture seems too thick. Chill.

◆ Serve as a dip with corn chips, warmed pitta (pita) bread or crisp raw vegetables cut into bite-sized chunks.

NOTE Guacamole will discolour if not eaten soon after it is made. It can, however, be kept in the refrigerator for up to 2 hours if sprinkled with lemon juice and covered with cling film (plastic wrap) actually touching the surface.

◆ CHICKEN LIVER KEBABS ◆

INGREDIENTS

SERVES 3-4

450 g/1 lb chicken livers, filaments removed and cut into bite-sized pieces

15 ml/1 tbsp lemon juice

5 g/1 tsp paprika

2.5 g/½ tsp chilli (chili) powder

5 g/1 tsp cumin

5 g/1 tsp salt

1 sweet green (bell) pepper, cored, seeded and quartered

1 small Spanish (Bermuda) onion

45 ml/3 tbsp oil

30 g/2 tbsp chopped fresh coriander

PREPARATION

◆ Sprinkle the chicken livers with lemon juice and leave to stand for 10 minutes.

◆ Combine the paprika, chilli (chili) powder, cumin and salt.

◆ Blanch the pepper quarters in boiling water for 3 minutes, then refresh in cold. Drain and cut into 2.5 cm (1 in) squares.

◆ Pat the liver dry and sprinkle with the spice mixture. Thread onto flat skewers, alternating with pieces of pepper and onion.

◆ Grill (broil) or barbecue at a high heat, as close to the heat source as possible. Turn them occasionally and baste with the oil until browned but still pink in the middle — not more than 5 minutes.

◆ Serve immediately, sprinkled with fresh coriander.

❖ SEVICHE ❖

SERVES 4

450 g/1 lb firm white fish fillets (filets), skinned and cubed

½ cup/100 ml/4 fl oz lime juice

1 small onion, finely chopped

1 large tomato, peeled, seeded and chopped

1-2 fresh green chillies (chilies), seeded and thinly sliced

45 ml/3 tbsp olive oil

Salt

1 small ripe avocado, peeled, pitted and sliced (optional)

PREPARATION

◆ Put the fish into a pretty glass bowl, pour over it the lime juice, cover and leave to marinate for 4 to 6 hours or overnight.

◆ Half an hour or so before serving, stir in the remaining ingredients, except for the avocado, and season to taste.

◆ Chill briefly, and serve decorated with avocado slices, if you like.

In this Mexican speciality the lime juice 'cooks' the fish.

❖ MELON WITH CURRY MAYONNAISE ❖

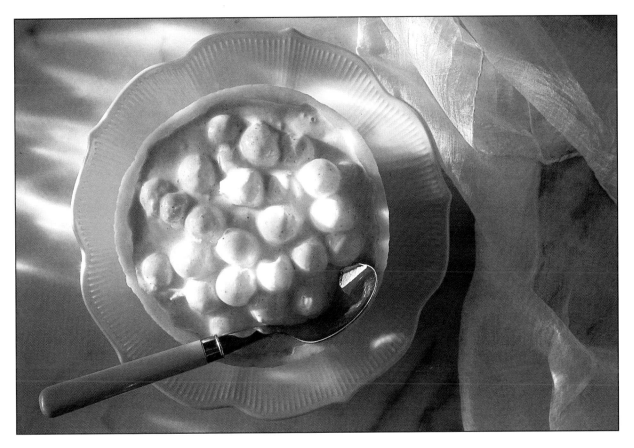

INGREDIENTS

SERVES 4

2 ripe, pink-flesh melons about 350 g/12 oz each

Approx. ½ cup/150 ml/¼ pt mayonnaise

15-30 ml/1-2 tbsp single (light) cream

Curry paste (bought or see recipe) to taste

A little lime or lemon juice

PREPARATION

➤ Halve the melons and scrape out the seeds. Either scoop out most of the flesh with a melon baller, or use a spoon and cut the flesh into bite-sized chunks. Turn the shells upside down to drain.

➤ Mix the mayonnaise with the cream (you might need more cream if the mayonnaise is very thick and home-made) and add curry paste and lime or lemon juice to taste. The dressing should be delicate.

➤ Combine the melon flesh with the dressing, pile back into the shells and chill before serving.

◆ DEVILLED CHICKEN WINGS ◆

SERVES 3 – 4
30 ml/2 tbsp oil
1-2 cloves garlic, crushed (minced)
15 ml/1 tbsp Worcestershire sauce
15 ml/1 tbsp tomato ketchup
5 g/1 tsp sugar
Good pinch salt
10 g/2 tsp English mustard
15 ml/1 tbsp lemon juice
12 chicken wings
Seasoned flour
Fat or oil for frying

PREPARATION

◆ Combine the oil, garlic, Worcestershire sauce, tomato ketchup, sugar, salt, mustard and lemon juice.

◆ Make several diagonal slashes in the fleshy part of each chicken wing and put them into a strong polythene bag. Pour in the marinade and tie the top of the bag. Put it on a plate in case of leaks and leave for several hours, turning it from time to time.

◆ Remove the chicken wings from their marinade drain and roll in seasoned flour.

◆ Fry them in a little hot fat or oil for 10 minutes or so, turning occasionally, until evenly browned and cooked through.

◆ Serve hot or warm with Avocado Cream Sauce (see recipe).

◆ As these are best eaten with your fingers, have some paper napkins handy.

VARIATION Instead of frying the chicken wings, they can be grilled (broiled) — no seasoned flour coating is needed — and basted in their marinade.

❖ Baked Avocado Crab ❖

INGREDIENTS

SERVES 4

1 tbsp/15 g/¹/₂ oz butter

15 g/¹/₂ oz flour

³/₄ cup/175 ml/6 fl oz hot milk

5 g/1 tsp grated Parmesan cheese

5 g/1 tsp tomato purée (paste)

200 g/7 oz canned or frozen crabmeat, flaked

Salt and Tabasco to taste

2 ripe avocado pears

OVEN TEMPERATURE: 175°C/325°F/GAS 4

PREPARATION

◆ Melt the butter over a moderate heat. Add the flour and cook for a minute, taking care not to let it brown. Gradually stir in the hot milk, then let the sauce simmer for 4 minutes to cook the flour.

◆ Off the heat, add the Parmesan, tomato purée (paste) and crabmeat and season to taste.

◆ Halve the avocados and discard the seeds. Remove about 10 g/2 tsp flesh from each half, mash finely and add to the crab mixture.

◆ Pile this into the avocado halves, arrange them in a baking dish and cook in a preheated oven until heated through and just beginning to brown, about 20 minutes.

◆ Serve immediately.

VARIATION If you are using fresh crabmeat, simmer the shell in a little water and white wine and use some of this stock to replace half the milk when making the sauce.

◆ POTTED SHRIMPS ◆

INGREDIENTS

SERVES 4
75 g/3 oz butter
550 g/1¼ lb (one pint) cooked shrimps
5 g/½ tsp freshly ground black pepper
Pinch of cayenne
2.5 g/½ tsp ground mace
Salt to taste
30 ml/2 tbsp single (light) cream
Brown toast
Lemon wedges

PREPARATION

◆ Melt one-third of the butter in a frying pan (skillet) and toss the shrimps, spices and seasoning over a moderate heat for 3 minutes.

◆ Add the cream, check seasoning and pack into individual pots or ramckin dishes. Pour over the rest of the butter, melted and skimmed. Chill.

◆ Serve with triangles of crisp brown toast and lemon wedges.

◆ BURRITOS ◆

INGREDIENTS

SERVES 6-8
1 recipe Flour Tortillas (see recipe)
1 recipe Guacamole (see recipe)
1 recipe Tomato Chilli (Chili) Sauce (see recipe)
300 g/10 oz canned refried beans, heated
½ recipe Mexican Tomato Salad (see recipe)
1 small crisp lettuce, shredded
1 medium sweet Spanish onion, cut into rings
1 large red or green pepper, cored, seeded and sliced
225 g/8 oz Cheddar cheese, shredded or grated
¾ cup/150 ml/6 fl oz thick sour cream or crème fraîche

This favourite Mexican snack consists simply of a hot Flour Tortilla (see recipe) wrapped around a filling — hot, cold, delicate, highly spiced or a combination. As they are best eaten with your fingers, do have a pile of paper napkins handy.

To get your imagination going, try the above, served in separate bowls — the hot foods, perhaps, on spirit burners — so that your guests can help themselves.

Avocado Chilli (Chili) Tart

◆ AVOCADO CHILLI (CHILI) TART ◆

INGREDIENTS

PREPARATION

SERVES 6

1½ cups/150 g/6 oz plain (all-purpose) flour

5 g/1 tsp paprika

Pinch salt

½ cup/100 g/4 oz butter

1 egg yolk

A little ice water

1 cup/300 ml/½ pt Tomato Chilli (Chili) Sauce (see recipe), chilled

2 ripe avocados, peeled and sliced lengthwise

Lemon juice

45 ml/3 tbsp thin sour cream

45 g/3 tbsp chopped fresh coriander or parsley

OVEN TEMPERATURE: 200°C/400°F/GAS 6

◆ Sift together the flour, paprika and salt. Rub in the butter until the mixture resembles fine bread-crumbs. Add the egg yolk and enough ice water just to hold the dough together.

◆ Press the pastry (it will be too fragile to roll) into a 22 cm (9 in) flan tin. Line the pastry with buttered foil, fill with dried beans and bake for about 20 minutes.

◆ Remove the foil and beans and return pastry to the oven for a further 5 minutes to brown.

◆ Carefully remove the pastry from its tin while still warm and set to cool on a wire rack.

◆ Put the pastry shell on a serving plate and spread the chilled Tomato Chilli (Chili) Sauce over the bottom. Top with avocado slices.

◆ Sprinkle with a little lemon juice, swirl on the cream (thinned, if necessary, with a little lemon juice), sprinkle with chopped coriander or parsley and serve immediately, accompanied by Avocado Cream Sauce (see recipe), if you like.

◆ MEXICAN STUFFED PEPPERS ◆

INGREDIENTS

PREPARATION

SERVES 4

5 medium crisp green or red (bell) peppers

1 fresh green chilli (chili), seeded and chopped

1 small onion, finely chopped

30 ml/2 tbsp olive oil

½ cup/100 ml/4 fl oz water

15 g/1 tbsp tomato purée (paste)

2.5 g/½ tsp dried oregano

¼ cup/50 ml/2 fl oz lime juice

Salt, pepper and sugar to taste

FILLING

2 fresh green chillies (chilies), or canned jalapeño peppers (these are hot)

15 ml/1 tbsp olive oil

1 large onion, thinly sliced

1 cup/225 g/8 oz cream cheese

60 g/4 tbsp pomegranate seeds (optional)

◆ Prepare the peppers a day in advance. Char 4 of them evenly over a gas flame or under the grill (broiler) until the skin blisters. Wrap in a tea (dish) towel and leave to cool, then rub off the skins under running water. Slit each pepper down one side and carefully cut out the cores and remove the seeds.

◆ Fry the chillies (chilies) in the oil with the onion until softened, then add the water, tomato purée (paste), oregano, lime juice and seasoning. Simmer for 5 minutes, add the prepared peppers and cook for 10 minutes, turning once, until just tender.

◆ Remove the peppers to a serving dish. Boil up the marinade vigorously until it reduces to a few tablespoonfuls, pour over the peppers, cover and refrigerate overnight.

◆ To make the filling, char, seed and chop the remaining pepper, and seed and slice the chillies (chilies) finely lengthways.

◆ Heat the oil and soften the onion, chillies and pepper for about 10 minutes. Cool.

◆ Stir in the cream cheese and two-thirds of the pomegranate seeds, if used, and season to taste.

◆ Stuff the peppers and serve chilled, sprinkled with the remaining pomegranate seeds if used.

◆ EGGS, CHEESE & PASTA ◆

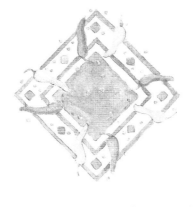

◆ EGG CURRY ◆

INGREDIENTS

SERVES 2

1 medium onion, chopped

1 clove garlic, crushed (minced)

½-1 fresh green chilli (chili), seeded and chopped

15 ml/1 tbsp ghee or oil

5 g/1 tsp ground turmeric

2.5 g/½ tsp fenugreek seeds

10 g/1½ tsp Garam Masala (bought or see recipe)

150 g/6 oz cauliflower florets (flowerets)

30 g/2 tbsp dessicated (dried) coconut

½ cup/100 ml/4 fl oz water

Salt to taste

4 hard-boiled (hard-cooked) eggs

PREPARATION

◆ Fry the onion, garlic and chilli (chili) in the ghee or oil until it just begins to brown. Add the spices and stir for a couple of minutes.

◆ Add the cauliflower and coconut and stir until well coated.

◆ Pour in the water, bring to the boil, then turn down the heat and simmer until the vegetables are tender but not mushy, about 10 minutes. Season to taste.

◆ Add the eggs, warm through and serve hot, either with rice or crusty bread and a green salad.

◆ MEXICAN OMELETTE (OMELET) ◆

INGREDIENTS

SERVES 2

Knob of butter

4 eggs, lightly beaten with a little seasoning

15 g/1 tbsp chopped spring (green) onion

1 fresh green chilli (chili), seeded and thinly sliced

30 g/2 tbsp cooked sweetcorn

75 g/3 oz Cheddar cheese, grated

½ ripe avocado, peeled and sliced

PREPARATION

◆ Melt the butter in an omelette (omelet) pan and pour in the eggs.

◆ Sprinkle on the spring (green) onion, fresh chilli (chili), sweetcorn and cheese.

◆ As soon as the cheese melts, arrange the avocado slices on one half of the omelette, fold over and serve immediately.

Cheese and Chilli (Chili) Blintzes

◆ CHEESE AND CHILLI (CHILI) BLINTZES ◆

MAKES 8

1 cup/100 g/4 oz plain (all-purpose) flour

Good pinch salt

1 egg

Approx. 1¼ cups/300 ml/½ pt milk

4 tbsp/50 g/2 oz butter

FILLING

225 g/8 oz cottage or curd cheese

1 egg yolk

1½-2 fresh green chillies (chilies), seeded and chopped

30 g/2 tbsp chopped parsley or chives

Salt and white pepper to taste

◆ First make the pancake batter. Sift the flour and salt into a bowl and make a well in it. Break in the egg, add a little of the milk and mix into the flour. Gradually mix in half of the remaining milk, stirring well, to form a smooth, thick batter.

◆ Melt half the butter over a gentle heat and add to the batter. Stir in the remaining milk, then chill the mixture for at least an hour.

◆ For the filling, mix the cottage or curd cheese, egg yolk, chillies (chilies), and parsley or chives and season to taste. Chill until needed.

◆ To cook the pancakes, rub a little butter over the bottom of a small, heavy pancake or omelette (omelet) pan. Over a high heat add a couple of tablespoonfuls of the batter and tilt the pan so that the batter is evenly spread. As soon as the underside is lightly browned, turn it out onto a plate and cover with a tea (dish) towel. Fry the remaining pancakes in the same way.

◆ To fill the pancakes put an eighth of the cheese mixture onto the middle of the cooked side of each pancake and fold over the sides and ends to make a parcel.

◆ To serve the blintzes, heat them through in the remaining butter over a moderate heat until golden.

◆ CHEESE SOUFFLE ◆

SERVES 4

3 tbsp/40 g/1½ oz butter

25 g/1 oz plain (all purpose) flour

5 g/1 tsp English mustard

5 g/1 tsp ground coriander

2.5 g/½ tsp ground cumin

2.5 g/½ tsp freshly grated nutmeg

2.5 g/½ tsp sugar

1¼ cups/300 ml/½ pt hot milk

150 g/6 oz Cheddar cheese, grated

30 g/2 tbsp grated Parmesan cheese

Salt and white pepper to taste

Few drops Tabasco (optional)

6 eggs, separated

OVEN TEMPERATURE: 220°C/425°F/GAS 7

◆ Melt the butter over a moderate heat. Add the flour, mustard, spices and sugar and stir for a few minutes, not allowing the flour to brown.

◆ Gradually add the hot milk, then let the sauce simmer gently, stirring, for 4 minutes, to cook the flour.

◆ Off the heat, beat in the cheeses — they will melt into the sauce almost at once — and season with salt, white pepper and Tabasco, if you like. Beat in the egg yolks, one at a time.

◆ Whisk the egg whites with a pinch of salt until stiff. Beat a spoonful of white into the warm sauce to loosen it, then fold the sauce into the whisked whites.

◆ Pour into a well-greased 1¼ quart/1.25 l/2½ pt soufflé dish and bake for 25 to 35 minutes, depending on how creamy you like it in the middle.

◆ Serve immediately, perhaps with a tomato salad.

◆ TREBLE PEPPER EGGS ◆

INGREDIENTS

SERVES 2

1 medium onion, thinly sliced
1-2 cloves garlic, crushed (minced)
Pinch of chilli (chili) powder
30 ml/2 tbsp oil
2 sweet red (bell) peppers, cored, seeded and thinly sliced
2 tomatoes, skinned, seeded and chopped
1 canned pimiento (sweet red pepper) optional
Salt, pepper and sugar to taste
2 eggs
30 ml/2 tbsp single (light) cream
2 pinches paprika
OVEN TEMPERATURE: 200°C/400°F/GAS 6

PREPARATION

◆ Fry the onion, garlic and chilli (chili) powder in the oil until the onion begins to brown. Add the sweet pepper and fry for another minute, then turn down the heat and cook, covered, until the onions are soft.

◆ Add the tomatoes, chopped pimiento (sweet red pepper), (if used), and seasoning and heat through.

◆ Divide the mixture between 2 small, well-greased baking dishes. Make a shallow depression on the surface of each and break in an egg.

◆ Pour over the cream, sprinkle with paprika and bake in a preheated oven for 6 to 8 minutes, until the egg whites are just set. Serve immediately.

◆ Tagliatelle with Chilli (Chili) and Herbs ◆

INGREDIENTS

SERVES 2

1 fresh red chilli (chili)
25 ml/1½ tbsp oil
1 medium onion, finely chopped
1 clove garlic, crushed (minced)
10 g/1½ tsp tomato purée (paste)
A good handful fresh oregano, basil or marjoram, finely chopped
150-225 g/6-8 oz fresh egg tagliatelle
1 large tomato (about 225 g/8 oz), skinned and chopped OR a 225 g/8 oz can of tomatoes, semi-drained
Salt, sugar and freshly ground black pepper to taste

PREPARATION

◆ First split the chilli (chili) and remove the seeds. Soak for an hour in cold salted water, rinse and slice thinly.

◆ Heat the oil and fry the onion, garlic and chilli (chili) until the onion just begins to brown. Stir in the tomato purée (paste) and 15 g/1 tbsp of your chosen fresh herb.

◆ Cook the tagliatelle in lots of boiling salted water until *al dente*.

◆ Meanwhile, add the tomato, fresh or canned, to the onion mixture, season and simmer for 3 to 4 minutes.

◆ Just before serving add the remaining oregano, basil or marjoram to the sauce and heat through for a moment or two.

◆ Stir the sauce into the drained pasta and serve immediately. If you would like cheese with this try Parmesan, freshly grated if possible.

◆ FISH ◆

◆ MALAYSIAN FISH CURRY ◆

INGREDIENTS

PREPARATION

SERVES 6

350 g/12 oz dessicated (dried) coconut

1¼ cups/300 ml/½ pt boiling water

675 g/1½ lb firm white fish

Salt and pepper

2 large onions, chopped

2 cloves garlic, chopped

5 g/1 tsp ground coriander

2.5 g/½ tsp ground cumin

2.5 g/½ tsp ground turmeric

5 g/1 tsp sugar

3-4 dried red chillies (chilies), soaked in hot water
OR 5-7½ g/1-1½ tsp chilli (chili) powder

10 g/½ tbsp tamarind pulp soaked in 60 ml/4 tbsp hot
water for 20 minutes, then squeezed out and discarded
OR 30 ml/4 tbsp lime juice

45 ml/3 tbsp oil

30 g/2 tbsp anchovy paste
OR blachan — (oriental fish paste)

◆ First make coconut milk by putting the dessi-cated coconut in a deep bowl and pouring on the boiling water. Leave to stand for 15 minutes, then squeeze out the liquid. Discard the coconut and leave the milk in the refrigerator until needed.

◆ Skin and bone the fish, chop into bite-sized pieces and season.

◆ In a liquidizer, food processor or mortar combine the onions, garlic, coriander, cumin, turmeric, sugar, dried chillies (chilies), or chilli (chili) powder and tamarind or lime juice and reduce to a thick paste. You may have to do this in two batches.

◆ Fry the mixture in the oil for a couple of minutes, then add the anchovy paste or blachan and cook for a further minute.

◆ Add the fish and coconut milk and simmer gently (do not allow to boil) for 7 to 10 minutes, or until the fish is done.

◆ Correct seasoning and serve hot with plain boiled rice.

◆ CORIANDER BAKED FISH ◆

INGREDIENTS

PREPARATION

SERVES 4

15 g/1 tbsp ground coriander

Pinch of chilli (chili) powder

2.5 g/½ tsp ground allspice

1 cup/225 ml/8 fl oz thick Greek yogurt

Finely grated rind and juice of a small orange

750 g/1½ lb fillet of white fish, skinned, or a whole fish

30-45 g/2-3 tbsp chopped fresh coriander

OVEN TEMPERATURE: 175°C/350°F/GAS 4

◆ Fry the spices in the oil for a minute or so to release the flavours.

◆ Off the heat, stir in the yogurt and orange rind and juice.

◆ Deeply score the fish and put it in a baking dish. Mask with the yogurt mixture. Cover and leave to marinate for 2 to 3 hours.

◆ Bake the fish, still in its yogurt coating, in a preheated oven for 30 to 45 minutes, depending on thickness.

◆ Serve hot, sprinkled with fresh coriander.

❖ FRIED SWORDFISH WITH ALMONDS ❖

INGREDIENTS

SERVES 4

4 swordfish steaks

A little chilli (chili) powder

Salt

75 g/3 oz almonds, blanched and sliced

40 g/1½ oz ghee or butter

30 ml/2 tbsp lime juice

PREPARATION

◆ Dust the fish steaks with chilli (chili) powder and salt to taste.

◆ Fry the almonds in the ghee or butter for a couple of minutes until golden. Drain and reserve.

◆ Fry the fish steaks for 4 minutes each side, then add the lime juice, cover, and cook for 10 minutes more.

◆ Serve on rice, topped with the almonds and with the pan juices poured over.

This can be made with any firm, lean fish steaks, but as swordfish becomes more widely available, it is well worth seeking out.

◆ SKEWERED FISH ◆

SERVES 4

2-3 dried red chillies (chilies)

Juice of 2 limes

15 ml/1 tbsp oil

450 g/1 lb firm white fish, filleted and skinned

2 small bananas (not too ripe)

Lime wedges

PREPARATION

◆ Soak the chillies (chilies) in hot water for half an hour, then rinse them, chop very finely and mix with half the lime juice and the oil.

◆ Chop the fish into 2.5 cm (1 in) chunks and arrange them in a single layer on a plate. Pour the chilli (chili) mixture over them and leave to marinate in a cool place (not the refrigerator) for an hour or two.

◆ Peel the bananas and cut them into 10 mm (⅓ in) slices; and sprinkle with the rest of the lime juice.

◆ Thread the marinated fish cubes onto flat skewers, alternating with banana slices.

◆ Grill (broil) or barbecue, turning frequently and basting with the remaining marinade, until the fish is just cooked.

◆ Serve immediately, with plain rice, a green salad and lime wedges.

◆ KEDGEREE ◆

INGREDIENTS

SERVES 4 TO 6

1 medium onion, finely chopped

30 ml/2 tbsp oil

5 g/1 tsp turmeric

10 g/1½ tsp Garam Masala (bought or see recipe)

150 g/6 oz long-grain rice

Approx. 2½ cups/600 ml/1 pt fish stock or water

300 g/10 oz cooked smoked fish, roughly flaked

Salt and white pepper

4 tbsp/50 g/2 oz butter, melted

2 hard-boiled eggs, roughly chopped

Fresh parsley, chopped

PREPARATION

◆ Fry the onion in the oil until it begins to brown.
◆ Add the spices and rice and cook for a minute more, stirring well to coat the grains.
◆ Pour in the stock or water, bring to the boil and simmer, covered, for 20 minutes or so, until all the water is absorbed and the rice is *al dente*.
◆ Add the fish and season.
◆ To serve, stir in the melted butter and chopped eggs over a moderate heat for a minute or two, correct seasoning and sprinkle with parsley.

VARIATION For a richer dish, add 45–60 ml/3-4 tbsp thick (heavy) cream with the butter.

GINGER PRAWN (SHRIMP) STIR-FRY

INGREDIENTS

SERVES 2

350 g/12 oz large raw prawns (shrimp)

4 cm (1½ in) fresh ginger, peeled and grated

Juice of 1 lime

15 ml/1 tbsp dry sherry

15 ml/1 tbsp oil

Pinch 5-spice powder

Salt, pepper and sugar to taste

PREPARATION

◆ Peel and de-vein the prawns (shrimp) and put them into a strong polythene (plastic) bag. Add the ginger, lime juice and sherry and tie the top of the bag securely. Put it into a bowl in case of leaks and leave it to marinate in a cool place (not the refrigerator) for 2 to 4 hours.

◆ Heat the oil in a wok or a large, heavy frying pan. Drain the prawns and stir-fry them for 2 to 3 minutes, depending on size, until just firm.

◆ Add the 5-spice powder and marinade and season to taste.

◆ Warm the sauce through and serve immediately.

◆ SHRIMP QUICHE WITH POPPYSEEDS ◆

INGREDIENTS

SERVES 6

1½ cups/150 g/6 oz plain (all-purpose) flour

Good pinch salt

5 g/1 tsp paprika

Pinch of cayenne

½ cup/100 g/4 oz butter, softened

1 egg yolk

30-45 g/3-4 tbsp poppyseeds

FILLING

3 eggs, lightly beaten

¾ cup/150 g/6 oz cream cheese

1 cup/225 ml/8 fl oz single (light) cream

225 g/8 oz frozen shrimps, thawed

3 blades mace, broken into small pieces

Salt and white pepper to taste

OVEN TEMPERATURES: 220°C/425°F/GAS 7, THEN
175°C/350°F/GAS 4

PREPARATION

◆ Sift together the flour, salt, paprika and cayenne and rub into it the butter until the mixture resembles fine crumbs. Add the egg yolk and poppyseeds, and press the dough — it will be too fragile to roll — into a 22 cm (9 in) flan tin.

◆ Line the pastry with foil, fill with dried beans and bake at the higher temperature for about 20 minutes. Remove the foil and beans and leave to cool.

◆ For the filling, blend the eggs into the cream cheese. Stir in the cream, shrimps and mace and season to taste.

◆ Pour this mixture into the pastry case and bake in a preheated oven at the lower temperature for 25 minutes or so, until just set but still slightly creamy. Serve warm.

◆ MOULES AU GRATIN ◆

INGREDIENTS

SERVES 2

Pinch of saffron threads

¼ cup/50 ml/2 fl oz hot water

1 kg/2¼ lb uncooked mussels in their shells

¼ cup/50 ml/2 fl oz white wine

½ small onion, chopped

½ bayleaf

2 tbsp/25 g/1 oz butter

15 g/½ oz plain (all-purpose) flour

½ cup/150 ml/¼ pt hot milk

Salt and white pepper to taste

15 g/1 tbsp fresh white breadcrumbs

5 g/1 tsp grated Parmesan cheese

OVEN TEMPERATURE: 200°C/400°F/GAS 6

PREPARATION

◆ Infuse the saffron threads in the hot water for half an hour.

◆ Scrub the mussels well and remove the 'beards'. Discard any that are the slightest bit open.

◆ Put the mussels in a large saucepan with the saffron infusion, wine, onion and bayleaf half, and simmer, covered, until the mussels open.

◆ Take the pan off the heat, strain off the liquid and reserve. Remove the mussels from their shells.

◆ Melt three-quarters of the butter, add the flour and cook for a moment or two. Gradually stir in the hot milk and ½ cup/150 ml/¼ pt of the mussel liquor. Season and simmer for 4 minutes.

◆ Off the heat, add the shelled mussels and divide the mixture between 2 individual gratin dishes.

◆ Sprinkle with the breadcrumbs and Parmesan, dot with the remaining butter and bake in a preheated oven for 10 minutes or so, until the topping is lightly browned. Serve immediately.

◆ FISH IN DEVILLED CREAM ◆

INGREDIENTS

SERVES 4

4 firm, white fish steaks

2 tbsp/25 g/1 oz butter

⅔ cup/150 ml/¼ pt chilled cream, whipping or half double (heavy)

5 g/1 tsp English mustard

15 ml/1 tbsp Worcestershire sauce

Salt and Tabasco to taste

15 g/1 tbsp chutney (optional)

OVEN TEMPERATURES: 175°C/350°F/GAS 4, THEN 220°C/425°F/GAS 7

PREPARATION

◆ Arrange the fish steaks in a greased baking dish, dot with butter, cover the whole dish with foil and bake at 175°C/350°F/Gas 4 until the fish is just firm and flakes easily, about 25 minutes.

◆ Whip the cream. Lightly stir into it the mustard and Worcestershire sauce and season with a little salt and plenty of Tabasco. Finally fold in the chutney, if used.

◆ Mask the cooked fish steaks with the devilled cream and increase the heat to 220°C/425°F/Gas 7; bake for about 7 to 10 minutes. Serve immediately.

VARIATION Almost any cooked fish can be served this way, also slices of cooked chicken or turkey.

✦ MEAT ✦

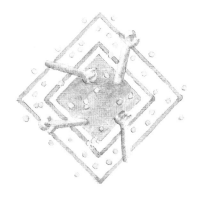

◆ PICADILLO ◆

INGREDIENTS

SERVES 4

1 medium onion, chopped

1 clove garlic, crushed (minced)

15 ml/1 tbsp oil

450 g/1 lb lean minced (ground) beef

3 large tomatoes, peeled, seeded and chopped
OR a 550 g/15 oz can, chopped

1 small apple or pear, peeled, cored and chopped

15 g/1 tbsp tomato purée (paste)

2 canned jalapeño chillies (chilies)
OR 2 fresh green chillies, seeded and chopped

2.5 g/½ tsp sugar

2.5 g/½ tsp ground cumin

Pinch of cinnamon

Pinch of cayenne

Pinch of ground nutmeg

Salt and pepper

30 g/2 tbsp chopped candied citrus peel

50 g/2 oz raisins

50 g/2 oz almonds, blanched and chopped

PREPARATION

◆ Soften the onion and garlic in the oil until they begin to brown.

◆ Turn up the heat and add the meat. Cook, stirring, until the meat is no longer pink.

◆ Add the tomatoes, apple or pear, tomato purée (paste), chillies (chilies), sugar and spices and season to taste. Simmer until the meat is cooked, about 20 to 25 minutes.

◆ Add the peel, raisins and almonds and cook a little longer.

◆ Serve hot over rice or pasta.

◆ PRESSED PEPPER FILLET (FILET) ◆

INGREDIENTS

SERVES 4 — 5

15 ml/1 tbsp oil

Thick piece beef fillet (filet), weighing about 900 g/2 lb

15 g/1 tbsp English mustard

Approx. 50 g/2 oz black peppercorns, coarsely crushed

OVEN TEMPERATURE: 230°C/450°F/GAS 8

PREPARATION

◆ Heat the oil in a frying-pan (skillet). Fry the beef quickly on all sides, to seal — this should take no more than 2 minutes.

◆ Smear the mustard over the beef and roll it in the crushed peppercorns; pressing so they adhere. Wrap tightly in foil and chill for at least 2 hours.

◆ Put the fillet (filet) in a roasting pan, still in its foil, and cook in a preheated oven for 25 minutes.

◆ Transfer the fillet to a board and loosen the foil, taking care not to disturb its pepper crust. Put another board or a plate on top, weighted with 3 × 450 g/1 1lb cans, and leave in the refrigerator overnight.

◆ Serve cut into 4 mm/⅙ in slices, perhaps with a salad of new potatoes.

Though purists may shudder, the combination of chilled rare beef and fiery but aromatic peppercorns is simply sensational. These can be scraped off just before serving: their fragrance will have permeated the meat.

◆ SOUZOUKAKLIA ◆

INGREDIENTS

SERVES 6

675 g/1½ lb minced (ground) beef, not too lean

1 medium onion, grated

Small bunch parsley, finely chopped

2.5 g/½ tsp cayenne

2.5 g/½ tsp cinnamon

5 g/1 tsp allspice

2.5 g/½ tsp ground coriander

Pinch ground nutmeg

2.5 g/½ tsp sugar

50 g/2 oz raisins (optional)

Salt and pepper to taste

A little oil

Lemon wedges

PREPARATION

◆ Combine all the ingredients except the oil and lemon wedges and mash to a paste. An electric mixer or food processor is useful for this.

◆ Shape into flattened sausages on flat, wide-blade skewers.

◆ Brush with oil and either grill (broil) or barbecue until browned, but still slightly pink in the middle.

◆ Slide off their skewers and serve on rice or in pockets of warm pitta (pita) bread, accompanied by lemon wedges.

A tasty Greek cross between a hamburger and a kebab.

◆ STIR-FRIED SZECHUAN BEEF ◆

INGREDIENTS

SERVES 2–3

350 g/12 oz (trimmed weight) lean steak
25 ml/1½ tbsp light vegetable oil
10 ml/½ tbsp light soy sauce
15 g/1 tbsp finely chopped spring (green) onion
5 g/1 tsp whole Szechuan pepper, lightly bruised
Salt to taste
5 ml/1 tsp sesame oil

PREPARATION

◆ Chill the beef well. Slice into 10 × 1 cm (4 × 1 in) strips, no more than 3 mm (⅙ in) thick.

◆ Combine two thirds of the vegetable oil with the soy sauce and spring (green) onion, mix into the meat and leave to marinate, covered, for 2 hours.

◆ Heat the remaining oil in a wok or heavy frying pan and toss the Szechuan pepper in it for 30 seconds. Add the meat and its marinade and stir fry until just cooked, no more than 3 minutes.

◆ Off the heat, stir in the sesame oil and serve immediately, perhaps with buttered egg noodles.

Szechuan pepper, also known as Fegara, is a speckled brown spice available from Chinese stores.

◆ FIREHOUSE CHILLI (CHILI) ◆

INGREDIENTS

SERVES 4

2 medium onions, chopped
2 cloves garlic, finely chopped
45 ml/3 tbsp oil
450 g/1 lb minced (ground) beef, not too lean
40 g/1½ tbsp chilli (chili) powder
10 g/2 tsp paprika
10 g/2 tsp ground cumin
30 ml/2 tbsp tomato ketchup
30 g/2 tbsp tomato purée (paste)
425 g/15 oz can of tomatoes, seeded
1½ cups/350 ml/12 fl oz lager (beer)
5 g/1 tsp sugar
5 g/1 tsp salt

Perhaps the hottest thing about the classic Chilli (Chili) is the argument about precisely what goes into it and in what proportions. In this recipe the long cooking time mellows the chilli powder and gives the sauce extra richness.

PREPARATION

◆ Soften the onions and garlic in the oil, then turn up the heat, add the beef and stir until it loses its pinkness.

◆ Add the spices, ketchup, tomato purée (paste), tomatoes and lager (beer).

◆ Simmer gently, uncovered, for an hour, stirring from time to time.

◆ Add salt and sugar and cook for a further hour, stirring occasionally.

◆ Correct seasoning and serve. This is good with plain rice or as a filling for Burritos (see recipe).

◆ Chilli (chili) is even better the next day. You will need to add extra liquid when reheating.

VARIATIONS You can add beans to this if you like; a drained 425 g/15 oz can of red kidney beans is fine, though you will need to add extra liquid.

◆ For Schoolhouse Chilli (Chili) — not as innocent as it sounds — simply halve the quantity of chilli (chili) used, or substitute mild chilli (chili) powder for the hot.

◆ KASHMIRI LAMB CURRY ◆

INGREDIENTS

SERVES 4

3 tbsp/40 g/1½ oz ghee or butter

2.5 cm/1 in fresh ginger, scraped and grated or finely chopped

450 g/1 lb lamb, trimmed and cubed

5 g/1 tsp Garam Masala (bought or see recipe)

10 g/2 tsp ground coriander

Pinch chilli (chili) powder

1½ cups/300 ml/½ pt stock or water

½ cup/75 g/3 oz blanched almonds

Ice water

45 ml/3 tbsp double (heavy) cream

Salt to taste

PREPARATION

◆ Heat the ghee or butter in a heavy pan. Add the ginger and lamb and stir over high heat until the meat begins to brown.

◆ Add the garam masala, coriander and chilli (chili). Stir, then add the water. Bring to the boil and simmer until the lamb is just tender, about 25 minutes.

◆ Pulverize two-thirds of the almonds in a mortar, liquidizer or food processor, adding enough ice water to make a smooth paste. Stir in the cream.

◆ Add the almond mixture to the lamb and salt to taste. Cook very gently for a further 4 minutes.

◆ Serve hot, sprinkled with the remaining almonds, coarsely chopped.

◆ LITTLE LAMB PIES ◆

INGREDIENTS

PREPARATION

SERVES 8

20 g/¾ oz fresh yeast

5 g/1 tsp sugar

Approx. 1¼ cups/300 ml/½ pt warm water

450 g/1 lb plain (all-purpose) flour

5 g/1 tsp salt

30 ml/2 tbsp olive oil

FILLING

50 g/2 oz pine kernels (pine nuts; pignoli)

15 ml/1 tbsp oil

1 medium onion, grated and squeezed out

450 g/1 lb minced (ground) lamb

1 ripe tomato, peeled, seeded and finely chopped

A good handful of parsley, flat-leaved if possible, finely chopped

30 ml/2 tbsp lemon juice

2.5 g/½ tsp sugar

2.5 g/½ tsp ground allspice

Pinch of cayenne

Salt and freshly ground black pepper

OVEN TEMPERATURE: 230°C/450°F/GAS 8

◆ First make the dough. Cream the yeast with the sugar. Add a little of the water and leave to stand for 5 minutes.

◆ Sift the flour and salt into a mixing bowl and make a well in it. Pour in the yeast mixture, oil and enough water to make a stiffish dough, and mix.

◆ Knead this on a lightly floured surface for 15 minutes or so, until smooth and elastic. Put it in an oiled bowl, cover with a tea (dish) towel and leave to stand in a warm place until doubled in size, anything from 1 to 2 hours.

◆ Punch down the dough and divide into 8 pieces. Roll each piece into a ball, cover with a cloth and leave to rise for 30 minutes more.

◆ Meanwhile make the filling. Fry the pine kernels (nuts) in the oil until lightly gilded.

◆ Turn them into a bowl, add the remaining ingredients and mix thoroughly. Season well.

◆ Roll out the dough-balls into rounds 10 cm (4 in) across and arrange on oiled baking trays (cookie sheets), allowing room for them to expand.

◆ Pile an eighth of the filling onto each and spread to within about 1 cm (½ in) of the edge.

◆ Bake the pies in a preheated oven for half an hour or so, until the dough is just browned. Serve either hot or warm.

This Syrian speciality — more pizza than pie — is traditionally served with a bowl of chilled yogurt. Tomato Chilli (Chili) Sauce (see recipe) would be equally good.

❖ RUBY RIBS ❖

SERVES 4

15 kg/3 lb wing or sheet pork ribs

60 g/4 tbsp apricot jam, warmed

5-10 g/1-1½ tsp chilli (chili) powder

5 g/1 tsp 5-spice powder

30 ml/2 tbsp soy sauce

30 ml/2 tbsp lemon juice

1¼ cups/300 ml/½ pt stock or water

OVEN TEMPERATURES: 165°C/325°F/GAS 3, THEN
230°C/450°F/GAS 8

PREPARATION

◆ Separate the ribs and arrange them in a single layer in a roasting tin.

◆ Mix the apricot jam, chilli (chili) powder, 5-spice powder, soy sauce and lemon juice. Gradually add the stock or water, stirring well.

◆ Pour the liquid over the ribs, cover the whole tin with foil and bake in a preheated oven at 165°C/325°F/Gas 3 for 1½ hours. The meat should be really tender and succulent.

◆ Pour the liquid off into a saucepan and boil over a high heat, stirring, until sticky and much reduced. Paint this glaze over the ribs and roast them, uncovered at 230°C/450°F/Gas 8, turning once, until the outside is crisp, about 10 to 15 minutes.

VARIATION The glazed ribs can also be grilled (broiled) or barbecued. Baste them with a little oil.

◆ SINGAPORE COCONUT PORK ◆

INGREDIENTS

SERVES 4

2 cups/425 ml/15 fl oz boiling water

225 g/8 oz dessicated (dried) coconut

1 large onion, grated

10 g/1½-2 tsp chilli (chili) powder

45 ml/3 tbsp coconut oil or ghee

450 g/1 lb lean pork, cubed

1 stem lemongrass, bruised (optional)

15 ml/1 tbsp lime juice

Sugar and salt to taste

PREPARATION

◆ First make coconut milk by pouring the boiling water over the coconut, leaving it to stand for 15 minutes, then squeezing out the liquid. Refrigerate until needed.

◆ Fry the onion and chilli (chili) powder in the oil or ghee for a few moments without browning. Add the pork and fry until the meat is browned and well coated with the onion and chilli (chili) mixture. Turn down the heat and stir in the coconut milk. Add the lemongrass, if used. Add salt to taste, cover and simmer gently until the pork is tender.

◆ Remove the lemongrass, add the lime juice and a little sugar and serve hot with plain boiled rice.

◆ PORK IN CHILLI (CHILI) SAUCE ◆

INGREDIENTS

SERVES 6

675 g/1½ lb stewing pork, trimmed and cubed

1 small onion, quartered

1 whole clove garlic, peeled

A bouquet garni

SAUCE

15 g/1 tbsp chilli (chili) powder

50 g/2 oz blanched almonds

30 ml/2 tbsp oil

2 large tomatoes, seeded and chopped

2 cloves garlic, crushed (minced)

1 large onion, chopped

2 canned pimientos (sweet red peppers), quartered

Salt and sugar to taste

15 ml/1 tbsp lime juice

2 sour apples, peeled, cored and chopped

2 thick slices fresh pineapple, cored and chopped

PREPARATION

◆ Put the pork in a saucepan with just enough water to cover. Add the onion, garlic clove and bouquet garni and simmer until tender, about 30 minutes. Drain, reserving the liquid.

◆ Meanwhile, fry the chilli (chili) powder and almonds in the oil until browned. Drain, reserving the oil, and blend or process to a smooth paste with the tomatoes, garlic, onion, pimientos (sweet red peppers) and a little meat stock.

◆ Fry the paste in the reserved oil over a high heat until thick. Season with salt and sugar and add the lime juice. Add the pork, the fruit and enough pork cooking liquid to give the sauce a coating consistency. Simmer until the apple is tender, about 10 minutes.

◆ Serve with plain boiled rice.

The Mexican recipe on which this is based is known as 'The Tablecloth Stainer' for obvious reasons.

◆ SPICY SAUSAGE PATTIES ◆

INGREDIENTS

MAKES 6

450 g/1 lb pork, minced (ground)

100 g/4 oz pork or bacon fat, minced (ground)

100 g/4 oz crustless white bread, soaked in water and squeezed out

2 cloves garlic, crushed (minced)

15 g/1 tbsp paprika

2.5 g/$\frac{1}{2}$ tsp ground white pepper

Pinch of cayenne

2 pinches ground nutmeg

2 pinches ground cloves

2 pinches ground cinnamon

15 g/1 tbsp tomato purée (paste)

15 ml/1 tbsp wine vinegar

2.5 g/$\frac{1}{2}$ tsp sugar

5 g/1 tsp salt

Oil for frying

PREPARATION

◆ Combine all the ingredients, either in an electric mixer or a food processor until thoroughly mixed. Check seasoning.

◆ Refrigerate, covered, for 24 hours, then shape into 6 patties.

◆ Fry in a little oil and serve with noodles or creamy mashed potatoes and a tomato sauce. These freeze well.

◆ PORTOBELLO CHICKEN VINDALOO ◆

INGREDIENTS

SERVES 4

4-6 fresh red chillies (chilies)

4 good-sized chicken portions, halved

60 ml/4 tbsp ghee or oil

1 large onion, chopped

3 cloves garlic, crushed (minced)

2.5 cm (1 in) fresh ginger, peeled and grated

10 g-2 tsp Garam Masala (bought or see recipe)

2.5 g/½ tsp fenugreek seeds

2.5 g/½ tsp ground turmeric

Juice of 1 lime

15-30 ml/1-2 tbsp vinegar

Approx. 1¼ cups/300 ml/½ pt chicken stock or water

Salt to taste

PREPARATION

◆ Split the chillies (chilies) and remove the seeds. Soak them in cold salted water for an hour or so, changing the water occasionally. Rinse them and mince finely.

◆ Brown the chicken pieces on all sides in the oil, drain and reserve.

◆ Fry the onion, garlic, spices and chilli (chili) in the oil remaining in the pan until the onion just begins to colour.

◆ Add the remaining ingredients and simmer, covered, until the chicken is tender, about 45 to 55 minutes. You may need to add a little more liquid.

◆ Add salt to taste and serve with plain boiled rice, a selection of chutneys and a cooling salad.

This streamlined version of the Indian classic is hot, so do warn your guests. If in doubt, use fewer chillies (chilies) — you can always add some Pepper Wine (see recipe) to hot things up.

POUSSIN (CORNISH GAME HEN)
IN A PEANUT CHILLI (CHILI) CRUST

INGREDIENTS

SERVES 4

4 fresh poussins (Cornish game hens), about 450 g/1 lb each

2 limes

5 cm/2 in fresh ginger, peeled and grated

30 ml/2 tbsp oil

CRUST

100 g/4 oz shelled peanuts

1 small onion, finely chopped

2.5–5 g/½-1 tsp chilli (chili) powder

2.5 g/½ tsp ground cumin

30 ml/2 tbsp oil

15 ml/1 tbsp light soy sauce

15 g/1 tbsp soft, dark brown sugar

Finely grated rind and juice of 1 lime

Extra lime wedges (optional)

OVEN TEMPERATURE: 190°C/375°F/GAS 5

PREPARATION

Score two shallow diagonal slashes on each poussin (Cornish game hen) breast and thigh. Pare one of the limes thinly and squeeze both of them. Push a quarter of squeezed-out lime inside each bird and put them into a strong polythene (plastic) bag.

For the marinade, combine the lime juice, ginger and oil and pour into the bag over the poussins. Add the pared lime peel, torn into small pieces. Securely tie the top of the bag, put it into a bowl in case of leaks and leave to stand at room temperature for 4 hours, or overnight in the refrigerator, turning occasionally.

For the crust, first toast the peanuts in a pre-heated oven, shaking the pan occasionally, until evenly browned. Tip out into a tea (dish) towel and rub off the skins, then either pound, liquidize or process them to the texture of fine crumbs.

Fry the onion, chilli (chili) powder and cumin in the oil for a minute or two, then add the soy sauce and brown sugar. Turn down the heat and add the peanuts and cook for a minute more, stirring well. Off the heat, add the grated lime rind and juice.

Lift the birds out of their marinade and arrange in a large roasting pan, breasts up.

Add the marinade, except for the pieces of lime peel, to the peanut mixture and smear over the birds. Cover with foil and bake in a preheated oven for 35 to 45 minutes, removing the foil halfway through.

The poussins (Cornish game hens) are done when clear as opposed to pink juices run when the thigh is pierced with a fork or skewer.

Serve with plain rice, a green salad and lime wedges, if you like.

If you wish to make a gravy for the poussins (Cornish game hens), deglaze the pan juices with a little water or thin cream and season to taste. Extra lime juice is a good addition, as is a spoonful of redcurrant jelly.

◆ TANDOORI CHICKEN ◆

INGREDIENTS

SERVES 4

2 spring (frying) chickens, weighing about
275 g/1½ lb each

1 medium onion, finely chopped

2 cloves garlic, crushed (minced)

2½ cm/1 in piece fresh ginger, grated

10 g/2 tsp chilli (chili) powder

15 g/1 tbsp Garam Masala (bought or see recipe)

10 g/2 tsp ground coriander

5 g/1 tsp ground cumin

15 ml/1 tbsp ghee or oil

½ cup/125 ml/¼ pt yogurt

30 ml/2 tbsp lemon juice

5 g/1 tsp salt

Lemon wedges

PREPARATION

◆ Skin the chickens and either halve or quarter them. Score the meat so that the marinade can penetrate more thoroughly.

◆ Fry the onions, garlic and spices in the ghee or oil for a minute or two to release the flavours. Stir into the yogurt. Add the lemon juice and salt and pour over the chicken.

◆ Rub the marinade well in, cover and leave to marinate for up to 24 hours, overnight is fine.

◆ Drain the chicken and grill (broil) or barbecue, with the meat as close as possible to the heat source, until the outside is crisp and browned and the inside is just cooked, but still juicy.

◆ Serve with lemon wedges.

❖ Simple Spiced Roast Chicken ❖

INGREDIENTS

SERVES 4

2.5 cm (1 in) fresh ginger, peeled and grated

Seeds from 4 cardamom pods, lightly crushed

10 g/2 tsp coriander seeds, dry fried for 30 seconds

Pinch of ground cloves

Pinch of ground allspice

Pinch of coarsely ground black pepper

5 g/1 tsp salt

3 tbsp/40 g/1½ oz butter, softened

1.6 kg/3½ lb roasting chicken

15 ml/1 tbsp oil

Rock salt

OVEN TEMPERATURE: 200°C/400°F/GAS 6

PREPARATION

◆ Grind or process the spices and salt, adding the butter bit by bit until well mixed.

◆ Work your fingers under the skin of the chicken, over the breast and thighs, carefully freeing it from the meat without tearing.

◆ Spread the spiced butter under the loosened skin and leave for 2 to 3 hours for the flavours to permeate.

◆ Put the chicken in a roasting pan, brush it with a little oil, sprinkle with rock salt, cover with foil and bake in a preheated oven for 45 minutes to an hour — until the juices no longer run pink — removing the foil for the last 20 minutes of cooking time to crisp the skin.

◆ SINGER CHICKEN ◆

INGREDIENTS

SERVES 4–6

4 chicken breast portions

45 g/3 tbsp mild French mustard

½ cup/100 ml/4 fl oz dry white wine

¼ cup/50 ml/2 fl oz water

½ lemon or 1 lime, thickly sliced

15 g/1 tbsp chopped fresh coriander

1 tbsp/12½ g/½ oz butter

15 ml/1 tbsp oil

10 g/2 tsp ground coriander

5 g/1 tsp ground cumin

2.5 g/½ tsp cayenne

150 g/6 oz small green grapes

150 ml/6 fl oz thick sour cream or crème fraîche

100 ml/4 fl oz thick yogurt

1 small can (approx. 150 g/6 oz) water chestnuts, drained

30 g/2 tbsp chopped fresh coriander or parsley to garnish

OVEN TEMPERATURE: 190°C/375°F/GAS 5

PREPARATION

◆ Put the chicken in an oven-proof dish and smear with two-thirds of the mustard. Add the wine, water, lemon or lime slices and coriander.

◆ Dot with the butter, cover with foil and bake for half an hour, or until the chicken is just cooked. Leave to cool in its juice, then skin it and cut or tear into bite-sized pieces.

◆ To make the sauce, heat the oil in a small pan, add the spices and fry for a minute or two.

◆ Take off the heat and add the sour cream or crème fraîche, yogurt and the remaining mustard. Chill.

◆ To serve, combine the chicken, the halved water chestnuts, the grapes and sauce, thinning if necessary with a little of the chicken juice, and top with coriander or parsley.

VEGETABLE DISHES & SALADS

◆ DAL DELUXE ◆

INGREDIENTS

SERVES 4–6

30 ml/2 tbsp ghee or oil

2 cloves garlic, crushed (minced)

1 large onion, chopped

2 fresh green chillies (chilies), seeded and finely chopped

5 g/1 tsp ground turmeric

15 g/1 tbsp ground coriander

10 g/½ tbsp ground cumin

150 g/6 oz orange split lentils, washed

15 g/1 tbsp tomato purée (paste)

30 ml/2 tbsp tomato ketchup

2½ cups/600 ml/1 pt chicken or vegetable stock (broth)
OR 2½ cups/600 ml/1 pt boiling water with a stock (bouillon) cube added

Salt, black pepper and sugar to taste

50 g/2 oz flaked (slivered) almonds, toasted

PREPARATION

◆ Heat the oil and fry the garlic, onion, chillies (chilies) and spices until lightly browned, about 5 minutes.

◆ Add the lentils, tomato purée (paste) and ketchup and stir until well mixed.

◆ Add stock (broth) or water and stock (bouillon) cube and bring to the boil. Season.

◆ Turn down the heat and simmer, stirring occasionally, for 35–45 minutes, until the lentils start to fall apart.

◆ Just before serving, correct seasoning and stir in the almonds.

◆ HARISSA CARROTS ◆

INGREDIENTS

SERVES 6

675 g/1½ lb carrots

2 cloves garlic, crushed (minced)

5 g/1 tsp ground coriander

2.5 g/½ tsp powdered caraway seeds

60 ml/4 tbsp oil

5 g/1 tsp harissa (Tunisian hot pepper paste), mixed with 75 ml/3 fl oz hot water

30 ml/2 tbsp lemon juice

30 ml/2 tbsp vinegar

10 g/2 tsp sugar

5 g/1 tsp salt

60 g/4 tbsp chopped fresh coriander or parsley

PREPARATION

◆ Scrape or peel the carrots, depending on age. Slice them into rounds and cook in lots of boiling water until just tender, 10 to 15 minutes. Drain.

◆ Fry the garlic and spices in the oil for a few minutes, then add the diluted harissa, lemon juice, vinegar, sugar and salt.

◆ Stir in the carrots and cook, covered, for a further 7 minutes, by which time the liquid will have reduced and the carrots absorbed its flavours.

◆ Serve hot or cold, sprinkled with coriander or parsley. This is particularly good with grilled fish.

◆ SCALLOPED POTATOES WITH HORSERADISH ◆

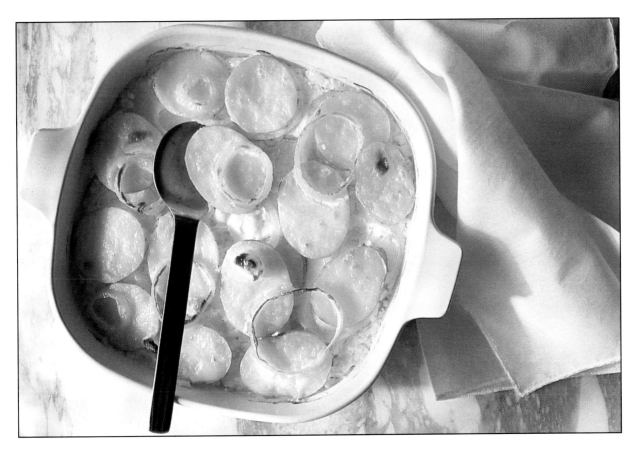

INGREDIENTS

SERVES 4–6

1 kg/2 lb potatoes, waxy new ones are good for this

1 small onion, thinly sliced

30 g/2 tbsp seasoned flour

30–45 g/2–3 tbsp freshly grated horseradish

1 cup/225 ml/8 fl oz single (light) cream

2 tbsp/25 g/1 oz butter

OVEN TEMPERATURE: 200°C/400°F/GAS 6

PREPARATION

◆ Scrub the potatoes — there is no need to peel them unless they are really old — and cut into 4 mm (⅙ in) slices.

◆ Cover the bottom of a well-greased gratin dish or small roasting pan with a layer of potato slices and a few pieces of onion and sprinkle with a little flour and horseradish.

◆ Repeat the layers until all the ingredients have been used, ending up with a layer of potatoes.

◆ Pour over the cream, dot with butter and bake in a preheated oven until the potatoes are tender, about 35 to 45 minutes, depending on thickness.

◆ Serve hot or warm with roast or grilled meat, particularly lamb.

◆ RED RICE ◆

INGREDIENTS

SERVES 4

1 medium onion, chopped

1 red pepper, seeded and chopped

2 canned pimientos (sweet red peppers), chopped

1 fresh red chilli (chili) OR 2½ g/½ tsp chilli (chili) powder

25 ml/1½ tbsp oil

10 g/2 tsp paprika

5 g/1 tsp ground cumin

150 g/6 oz long-grain rice, washed

15 g/1 tbsp tomato purée (paste)

2½ cups/600 ml/1 pt tomato juice

Salt, sugar and Tabasco to taste

PREPARATION

◆ Fry the onion, red pepper, pimientos and chilli (chili) in the oil until the onions begin to brown.

◆ Add the spices and rice and stir over a high heat for a minute or so until the rice is well coated.

◆ Add the tomato purée (paste), tomato juice and seasoning. Bring to the boil, then simmer, covered, for 20 to 25 minutes, until the rice is tender and the liquid absorbed.

◆ Serve hot with grilled (broiled) chicken or pork chops.

◆ SPICED POTATO AND CAULIFLOWER ◆

INGREDIENTS

SERVES 6
675 g/1½ lb potatoes
1 medium cauliflower
30 ml/2 tbsp oil
10 g/2 tsp ground cumin
15 g/1 tbsp finely chopped onion
Seeds from 3–4 cardamom pods
15 g/1 tbsp poppyseeds
Salt and lots of freshly ground black pepper

PREPARATION

◆ Peel the potatoes and cut them into 2.5 cm (1 in) chunks. Parboil in lots of salted water for 5 minutes, drain and reserve.

◆ Cut the cauliflower into bite-sized florets (flowerets), cover with cold water and leave to stand for half an hour.

◆ Heat the oil in a large frying pan and fry the cumin for 3 or 4 seconds, then add the onion and cardamom seeds and cook for a minute more.

◆ Add the potatoes and cauliflower — not too well drained as the water that adheres will cook the dish — and stir well to coat.

◆ Turn down the heat, cover the pan and cook, stirring from time to time, until the potatoes are cooked but the cauliflower still has a bit of crunch, 12 to 15 minutes.

◆ Stir in the poppy seeds, season to taste and serve hot.

VARIATION For Devilled Potato and Cauliflower, replace the cardamom and poppy seeds with 10 g/ 2 tsp dry English mustard and 2 good pinches cayenne.

Courgette (Zucchini) Fritters

◆ COURGETTE (ZUCCHINI) FRITTERS ◆

INGREDIENTS

SERVES 4
450 g/1 lb young courgettes (zucchini), no more than 2.5 cm/1 in thick
2 eggs
Pinch of cayenne
5 g/1 tsp dried oregano
Good pinch salt
Oil for shallow frying

PREPARATION

◆ Wash and trim the courgettes (zucchini). Halve them, then quarter them lengthwise.

◆ Make a batter by beating together the eggs, cayenne, oregano and salt until well mixed.

◆ Heat the oil in a frying pan (skillet).

◆ Dip the courgette (zucchini) pieces into the batter and fry, turning once, until crisp on the outside and tender in the middle. Drain on kitchen paper (paper towels) and serve hot.

VARIATION Aubergine (eggplant), sliced 6 mm (¼ in) thick, can also be cooked this way.

◆ SUNFLOWER SPINACH ◆

INGREDIENTS

SERVES 4
1 kg/2 lb fresh spinach
1 medium onion, finely chopped
45 ml/3 tbsp oil
1.25 cm/½ in fresh ginger, peeled and grated
5 g/½ tsp chilli (chili) powder
30 ml/2 tbsp water
45 g/3 tbsp seedless sultanas (golden raisins)
50 g/2 oz sunflower seeds

PREPARATION

◆ Wash the spinach and remove any tough stalks or discoloured leaves. Chop coarsely.

◆ Fry the onion in 30 ml/2 tbsp of the oil until lightly coloured. Add the spices and fry for a further minute, stirring well.

◆ Add the spinach, water and sultanas (golden raisins) and stir until well coated, then turn down the heat, cover and simmer for 5 minutes, stirring occasionally, by which time the liquid will have been absorbed and the spinach cooked.

◆ Fry the sunflower seeds in the remaining oil until golden, stir into the spinach and serve immediately.

◆ VEGETABLE CURRY ◆

INGREDIENTS

SERVES 4–6

1–2 fresh green chillies (chilies), seeded and chopped

2 cloves garlic, crushed (minced)

30 ml/2 tbsp ghee or oil

5 g/1 tsp ground turmeric

15 g/1 tbsp Garam Masala (bought or see recipe)

5 g/1 tsp mustard seed, crushed

5 g/1 tsp ground coriander

30 ml/2 tbsp lime or lemon juice

2 medium onions, chopped

1 large potato, peeled and cubed

450 g/1 lb mixed prepared vegetables, such as: cauliflower florets (flowerets); green (string or snap) beans, stringed and sliced; shelled peas; washed spinach, tough stems removed; etc.

2 ripe tomatoes, peeled and chopped

Approx. 1 cup/225 ml/8 fl oz water

Salt, pepper and sugar to taste

PREPARATION

◆ Fry the chillies (chilies) and garlic in the ghee or oil with the spices, and lime or lemon juice for 5 minutes.

◆ Add the onion, and stir over a high heat until it begins to brown.

◆ Add the vegetables, water and seasoning and simmer, uncovered and stirring occasionally, until the potato is cooked and most of the liquid evaporated — about 20 minutes. Serve hot.

❖ HONEY ONION PUREE ❖

INGREDIENTS

SERVES 4

450 g/1 lb onions, finely chopped

45 ml/3 tbsp oil

2.5 g/½ tbsp chilli (chili) powder

Pinch of cinnamon

2½ g/½ tsp powdered cubebs (optional)

1 g/¼ tsp powdered cloves

2.5 g/½ tsp ground allspice

2.5 g/½ tsp ground cumin

2.5 g/½ tsp ground turmeric

Salt to taste

45–60 ml/3–4 tbsp honey

PREPARATION

❖ Soften the onions in the oil, then add the spices and salt to taste. Cook, stirring from time to time, until the onions have collapsed into a purée.

❖ Add the honey and simmer for a few minutes more.

❖ Serve with grilled (broiled) or roast meat, particularly pork.

Cubebs or long pepper are a fairly rare spice, popular in the Renaissance period. More allspice can be substituted if they are unavailable.

◆ SAFFRON RICE AND ALMOND SALAD ◆

INGREDIENTS

SERVES 6

1 cup/225 g/8 oz long-grain rice

2½ cups/600 ml/1 pt water

Good pinch salt

2.5 g/½ tsp saffron threads infused for ½ hour
in 30 ml/2 tbsp hot water

2.5 g/½ tsp English mustard

15 ml/1 tbsp wine vinegar

45 ml/3 tbsp olive oil

5 g/1 tsp sugar

75–100 g/3–4 oz blanched almonds

1–2 fresh red chillies (chilies), seeded, rinsed and thinly
sliced (optional)

PREPARATION

◆ Put the rice, water, salt and saffron infusion in a saucepan, bring to the boil and simmer, covered, until the water has been absorbed and the rice is just tender, about 20 to 25 minutes. Take off the heat.
◆ Combine the mustard, vinegar, oil and sugar and stir into the hot rice. Chill.
◆ Just before serving, toast the almonds under the grill (broiler) or in a moderate oven, shaking the pan from time to time, until lightly browned. Stir into the chilled rice with the chillies (chilies), if used, and serve immediately. (If this salad is kept sitting around the almonds will lose their crunch.)

◆ CAULIFLOWER AND POMEGRANATE SALAD ◆

INGREDIENTS

SERVES 4–6

1 ripe avocado

45 ml/3 tbsp olive oil

15 ml/1 tbsp wine vinegar

5 g/1 tsp sugar

1 medium cauliflower (about 450 g/1 lb), broken into
small florets (flowerets)

Seeds from 2 pomegranates

50 g/2 oz walnuts, chopped (optional)

PREPARATION

◆ First make the dressing. Halve the avocado, discard the stone and scoop out the flesh into a mixing bowl, liquidizer or food processor.
◆ Add the oil, vinegar and sugar and mash or purée until smooth.
◆ Mix with the cauliflower and pomegranate seeds, stirring well to coat. Cover and chill for no more than half an hour.
◆ Serve sprinkled with walnuts, if liked.

This unusual salad may be neither hot nor spicy, but is a crisp and refreshing complement (and antidote) to dishes that are.

Saffron Rice and Almond Salad

Mexican Tomato Salad

INGREDIENTS

SERVES 4

1–2 fresh red chillies (chilies)

3 large tomatoes

3–4 spring (green) onions, finely chopped

Handful fresh coriander, finely chopped

15 ml/1 tbsp olive oil

10 ml/½ tbsp lime juice

Salt to taste

PREPARATION

Split and seed the chillies (chilies) and soak them in cold salted water for an hour. Rinse them and slice finely.

Peel the tomatoes. Loosen the skins by first pouring boiling water over them, letting them stand for 1 minute, then refreshing in cold. Halve the peeled tomatoes and scoop out the seeds. Either slice the flesh or cut into chunks.

Lightly stir in the rest of the ingredients, season and chill for half an hour before serving.

VARIATION Add 150–225 g/6–8 oz cubed or sliced mozzarella or feta cheese for a refreshing starter or a light lunch.

CURRIED PASTA SALAD WITH BANANAS

INGREDIENTS

SERVES 4

2 cups/225 g/8 oz dry pasta, spirals, bows or shells

10 ml/2 tsp oil

2 medium bananas, not too ripe

15 ml/1 tbsp lemon juice

15 ml/1 tbsp single (light) cream or milk

Curry paste (bought or see recipe) to taste

½ cup/150 ml/¼ pt mayonnaise

PREPARATION

Boil the pasta with the oil in lots of salted water until *al dente*. Drain.

Slice the bananas and sprinkle with the lemon juice.

Mix the cream and curry paste into the mayonnaise and combine with the warm pasta and bananas.

Serve warm or cold, with cold meats, curries or barbecues.

Gado-Gado

◆ GADO-GADO ◆

SERVES 4

1 cup/150 g/6 oz firm white cabbage, shredded
1 small onion, finely chopped
2 cloves garlic, crushed (minced)
15 ml/1 tbsp oil, preferably peanut
Pinch of chilli (chili) powder
1.25 cm/½ in fresh ginger, peeled and grated
30 g/2 tbsp peanut butter
Hot water
Salt and sugar to taste
150 g/6 oz bean sprouts
150 g/6 oz cucumber, peeled and cubed
50 g/2 oz salted peanuts (optional)
1 fresh green chilli (chili), seeded and thinly sliced (optional)

◆ Blanch the cabbage in lots of boiling salted water for 3 minutes, drain and leave to cool.

◆ Fry the onion and garlic in the oil until lightly browned, then add the spices and fry for a minute more.

◆ Turn down the heat and add the peanut butter and enough hot water to make the sauce a creamy consistency. Season to taste.

◆ Combine the cooled cabbage, bean sprouts and cucumber, pour over them the hot sauce and serve at once, garnished, if you like, with the peanuts and fresh chilli (chili).

◆ TABBOULEH WITH CHILLIES (CHILIES) ◆

SERVES 4

100 g/4 oz burghul (bulghur)
1 small onion, finely chopped
60 ml/4 tbsp lemon juice
5 g/1 tsp salt
1–2 fresh green chillies (chilies), seeded and thinly sliced
Generous handful fresh mint leaves, coarsely chopped
60 ml/4 tsp olive oil
Lettuce leaves (optional)

◆ Cover the burghul (bulghur) with cold water and leave to soak for 15 minutes, then drain in a fine sieve or a colander lined with a tea (dish) towel.

◆ Mix in the onion, lemon juice, salt and chillies (chilies) and combine well. Chill.

◆ To serve, stir in the mint and oil and, if you like, pile onto a bed of lettuce leaves.

◆ SAUCES ◆

◆ TOMATO CHILLI (CHILI) SAUCE ◆

INGREDIENTS

3–4 fresh red chillies (chilies)

2 medium onions, chopped

2 cloves garlic, crushed (minced)

30 ml/2 tbsp olive oil

45 g/3 tbsp tomato purée (paste)

5 g/1 tsp dried oregano

10 g/2 tsp paprika

5 g/1 tsp sugar

½ cup/100 ml/4 fl oz water or red wine

Salt to taste

PREPARATION

◆ Split and seed the chillies (chilies) and soak in cold, salted water for an hour or so, changing the water from time to time. Slice thinly.

◆ Fry the onion and garlic in the oil until just beginning to brown.

◆ Turn down the heat, add the chillies (chilies) and cook, covered, until the onions have softened, about 12 minutes.

◆ Add the tomato purée (paste), oregano, paprika, sugar and water or wine and simmer for a further 7 to 10 minutes, until the sauce has thickened slightly. Add salt to taste.

◆ Serve hot or cold.

◆ CHILLI (CHILI) MINT MARINADE ◆

INGREDIENTS

60 ml/4 tbsp good olive oil

A good handful fresh mint, chopped

5 g/1 tsp thyme, bruised

10 g/1½ tsp chilli (chili) powder

10 g/2 tsp salt

5 g/1 tsp ground black pepper

PREPARATION

◆ Score the meat and put it into a strong poly-thene (plastic) bag with the marinade ingredients. Tie the top of the bag and put it on a plate in case of leaks. Leave the meat to marinate for 2 to 4 hours, depending on size — a whole boned leg of lamb can be left overnight in the fridge. Turn the bag from time to time so that the marinade penetrates evenly.

◆ Use the remaining marinade for basting.

This uniquely North African combination of flavours is good with both lamb and chicken, grilled (broiled), spit-roasted or barbecued, and makes enough for 1.8 kg/4 lb meat.

◆ SATAY SAUCE ◆

INGREDIENTS

MAKES APPROX. 1½ CUPS/350 ML/
12 FL OZ

100 g/4 oz shelled raw peanuts

75 g/3 oz finely chopped onion

30 ml/2 tbsp oil

2.5 cm/1 in root ginger, peeled and grated

5 g/1 tsp chilli (chili) powder

30 g/2 tbsp soft, dark brown sugar

30 ml/2 tbsp soy sauce

30 ml/2 tbsp lemon juice

2.5 g/½ tsp 5-spice powder

¾ cup/175 ml/6 fl oz water

Salt to taste

OVEN TEMPERATURE: 175°C/350°F/GAS 4

PREPARATION

◆ Roast the peanuts in a preheated oven, shaking the pan occasionally, until lightly browned. Rub off the skins in a tea (dish) towel and return to the oven until a good deep tan. Cool and store in a polythene bag until needed.

◆ Just before you make the sauce, grind the peanuts coarsely in a food processor or wrap them loosely in a tough polythene bag and crush them with a steak hammer or a heavy saucepan.

◆ Brown the onion in the oil over a high heat. Add the ginger, chilli (chili) powder and peanuts and fry for a minute more, stirring.

◆ Turn down the heat, add the remaining ingredients and simmer for 5 minutes. Correct the seasoning and serve hot or warm with grilled or roasted meat, pork and chicken in particular.

VARIATIONS For a smoother sauce, or one suitable for marinating and basting grilled (broiled) or barbecued meats, especially kebabs, liquidize or process the cooked sauce. It should not be too smooth.

Coconut milk (for method see Singapore Coconut Pork) can be substituted for the water, in which case do not allow the sauce to boil.

◆ Aromatic Bread Sauce ◆

INGREDIENTS

SERVES 4–6

1 small onion

6–8 whole cloves

Scant 2 cups/450 ml/¾ pt milk

75 g/3 oz white bread, crusts removed

1 tbsp/12½ g/½ oz butter

A little salt and white pepper

Pinch of freshly grated nutmeg

30–45 ml/2–3 tbsp cream

PREPARATION

◆ Peel and halve the onion and stud each half with the cloves.

◆ Put the onion halves into a small heavy saucepan with the milk, bring to the boil and barely simmer for half an hour. Take off the heat and leave to cool.

◆ Squeeze the bread out in water and add to the milk, together with the butter and seasoning. Cook over a gentle heat for 15 to 20 minutes, stirring from time to time.

◆ Remove the onion, add the nutmeg and cream, correct seasoning and serve hot. This is equally good with roast chicken or baked ham.

VARIATION When you remove the onion before serving, you can take out the cloves, chop the onion finely and return it to the sauce with the nutmeg and cream.

If you have any sauce left over, it is excellent shaped into small patties, dipped in flour and fried in a little butter or oil, to serve with the cold roast next day.

◆ HARISSA SAUCE ◆

INGREDIENTS

MAKES APPROX. 1 CUP/225 ML/8 FL OZ
2–3 cloves garlic, crushed (minced)
30 ml/2 tbsp olive oil
10 g/1½ tsp ground cumin
30 g/1½ tbsp harissa paste
1 cup/225 ml/8 fl oz water
Salt to taste

PREPARATION

◆ Fry the garlic in the oil for a minute, then add the *harissa* and cumin and fry for a couple of minutes more.

◆ Add the water and salt to taste, bring to the boil and serve.

VARIATION 15 g/1 tbsp tomato purée (paste) and 2.5 g/½ tsp sugar can be added with the *harissa*.

This simple — and extremely hot — Tunisian sauce is best known as an accompaniment for couscous, but it goes well with most grilled (broiled) meats and fish and can even be used as a dip. Harissa paste can be bought in small cans at delicatessens and speciality stores selling Eastern and Middle East ingredients.

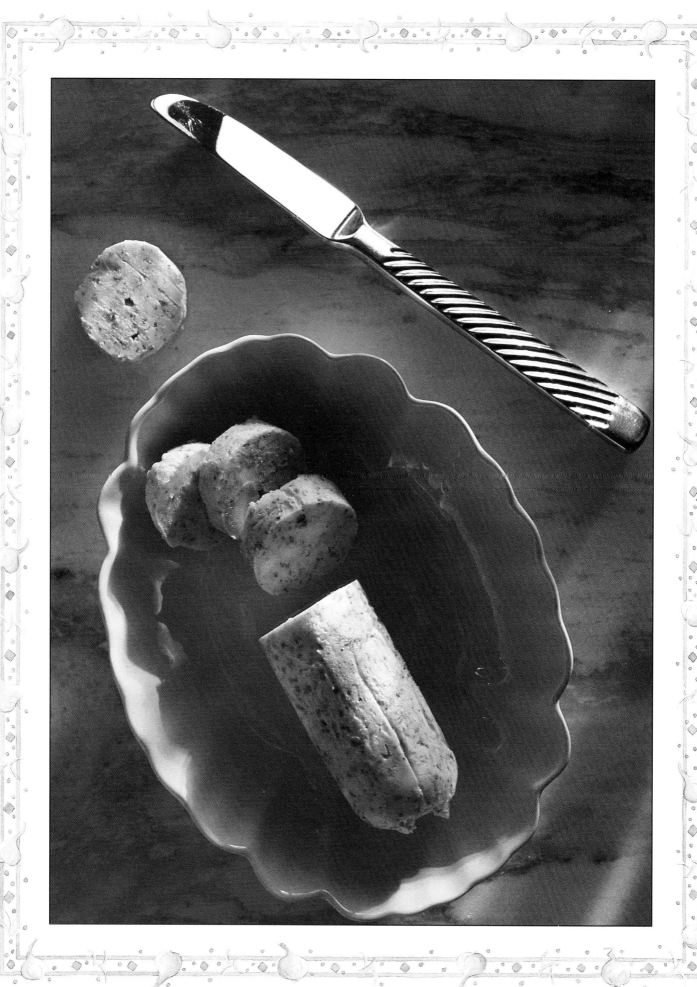

❖ CURRY BUTTER ❖

INGREDIENTS

MAKES ½ CUP/100 G/4 OZ
½ cup/100 g/4 oz butter, softened
1 clove garlic, finely crushed (minced)
Good pinch salt
2.5 g/½ tsp ground turmeric
15 g/1 tbsp Garam Masala (bought or see recipe) OR Curry Paste (see recipe) to taste
Cayenne to taste

PREPARATION

◆ Cream the butter until light and fluffy — warming the bowl helps.

◆ Work in the remaining ingredients and mix well. Wrap in foil and greaseproof (waxed) paper and chill or freeze until needed.

◆ For Curried Croutons, spread crustless slices of white bread generously with softened Curry Butter. Cut into small cubes and arrange, butter side up, on a baking tray (cookie sheet) and bake at a preheated 190° C/375° F/Gas 5 until crisp and golden. Unlike fried croutons, these can be kept warm without going soggy.

VARIATIONS To each ½ cup/100 g/4 oz creamed butter add:

For *Chilli (Chili) Butter:* 25 g/1 oz pounded canned pimiento, 10 g/2 tsp tomato purée (paste), 5 g/1 tsp chilli (chili) powder and salt to taste.

For *Devil Butter:* 15 ml/1 tbsp Worcestershire sauce, 15 ml/1 tbsp tomato ketchup, 2.5 g/½ tsp dry English mustard and salt and Tabasco to taste. 15 ml/1 tbsp chutney is a good addition, especially with sausages.

For *Mustard Butter:* 10 g/2 tsp dry English mustard OR 40 g/1½ tbsp French.

For *Coriander Butter:* 15 g/1 tbsp coriander seeds, warmed through in a moderate oven and ground, and the finely grated rind of an orange.

Savoury butters are a handy topping — virtually an instant marinade — for steaks, hamburgers, chops, and grilled (broiled) fish or chicken, and will enrich sauces, soups and stews. They also make sandwiches a lot more interesting.

◆ Fresh Apple and Horseradish Sauce ◆

INGREDIENTS

MAKES APPROX. 1 CUP/225 ML/8 FL OZ

1 sharp green dessert apple

5 ml/1 tsp lemon juice

½ cup/150 ml/¼ pt chilled cream, whipping or half double (heavy)

30 g/1½ tbsp freshly grated horseradish

PREPARATION

◆ Quarter and core the apple and grate it, without peeling it. Sprinkle it with lemon juice to prevent discolouration.

◆ Whip the cream to soft peaks and slightly stir in the grated apple and horseradish. Serve immediately.

❖ AVOCADO CREAM SAUCE ❖

INGREDIENTS

MAKES ABOUT 1¼ CUPS/300 ML/½ PT
1 large ripe avocado pear
15 ml/1 tbsp lime juice
125 ml/¼ pt thick sour cream or crème fraîche
15–30 g/1–2 tbsp chopped fresh coriander

PREPARATION

❖ Halve the avocados, discard the stone and scoop out the flesh.

❖ Mash, process or liquidize the avocado flesh with the remaining ingredients to a thick cream. Serve as soon as possible.

VARIATION For a bit more bite, add 2 chopped spring (green) onions and/or 10 g/½ tbsp French mustard and/or a few drops Tabasco.

This is also good if you substitute 75 ml/3 fl oz mayonnaise for the sour cream, especially served with prawns.

A deliciously cool sauce, especially good with chilli-based dishes.

◆ DESSERTS ◆

◆ CINNAMON TOAST ICE CREAM ◆

INGREDIENTS

SERVES 4–6

50 g/2 oz brown breadcrumbs

40 g/1½ oz brown sugar

10 g/1½ oz ground cinnamon

65 g/2½ oz white sugar

½ cup/100 ml/4 fl oz water

3 egg yolks, lightly beaten

5 ml/1 tsp vanilla essence (extract)

Scant 2 cups/450 ml/¾ pt chilled cream

OVEN TEMPERATURE: 200°C/400°F/GAS 6

PREPARATION

◆ Mix the breadcrumbs, brown sugar and cinnamon and bake for 20 to 25 minutes, until crisp and browned. As the crumbs will not brown evenly, take them out from time to time and fork those at the edges of the pan to the middle.

◆ Leave the cooked crumbs to cool in the tin (pan), then either grind or pound them coarsely and store in an airtight container until needed.

◆ To make the ice cream, dissolve the white sugar in the water over a low heat until the bottom of the pan no longer feels "gritty" when tapped with a wooden spoon.

◆ Turn up the heat and boil until a little of the syrup will draw out to a short thread between your forefinger and thumb. Take the pan off the heat and leave to stand for 30 seconds.

◆ Pour the hot sugar syrup onto the egg yolks, whisking all the while, and continue to whisk over cold water or ice cubes until the mixture pales, thickens and cools. Add the vanilla essence (extract).

◆ Whip the chilled cream to soft peaks and stir it into the egg mixture.

◆ Freeze the ice cream in a metal container, stirring from time to time to break down the ice crystals. When half frozen, beat it — easiest in an electric mixer — until smooth. Stir in most of the cinnamon crumbs. Pack and freeze until firm.

◆ Transfer the ice cream to the refrigerator half an hour before serving. Sprinkle each bowlful with the remaining crumbs.

CARDAMOM CRUMBLE WITH APRICOTS

INGREDIENTS

SERVES 4–6

225 g/8 oz dried apricots

8–9 cardamom pods

Approx. 1¼ cups/300ml/½ pt boiling water

5 g/1 tsp white sugar

¼ cup/50 g/2 oz butter, diced

½ cup/50 g/2 oz plain (all-purpose) flour, sifted

¼ cup/50 g/2 oz Demerara (light brown) sugar

A little lemon juice

OVEN TEMPERATURE: 200°C/400°F/GAS 6

A marvellously intense and fragrant finale for even the grandest dinner party.

PREPARATION

◆ Put the apricots and 6 or 7 of the cardamom pods in a saucepan and pour over them the boiling water. Cover and leave to soak for a couple of hours, or overnight, then simmer gently until the apricots are soft — between 25 and 45 minutes, depending on how dry the apricots were and how long they were soaked. Leave to cool.

◆ Remove the black seeds from the remaining cardamom pods and grind them with the white sugar in a spice or coffee grinder or pepper mill. Reserve.

◆ For the crumble topping, rub into the butter the flour, Demerara sugar and half the ground cardamom mixture until the mixture resembles coarse crumbs. Chill until needed.

◆ To assemble, discard the cooked pods and mash the apricots to a coarse purée. Add lemon juice to taste. Spread over the bottom of a lightly greased gratin dish or four individual ramekin dishes. The purée should be no more than 2 cm (¾ in) thick. Sprinkle the surface with the remaining ground cardamom mixture and top with the crumble.

◆ Bake in a preheated oven for 20 to 30 minutes, until the crumble topping is crisp and pale gold. Serve warm with lots of single (light) cream.

◆ CREOLE BANANAS ◆

INGREDIENTS

SERVES 4

6 medium bananas, ripe

3 tbsp/37½ g/1½ oz butter

¼ cup/50 g/2 oz Demerara (light brown) sugar

¼ cup/75 ml/3 fl oz dark rum

Approx. 15 ml/1 tbsp lime or lemon juice

Freshly grated nutmeg

OVEN TEMPERATURE: 175°C/350°F/GAS 4

PREPARATION

◆ Peel the bananas, halve them lengthwise and arrange them in a single layer in a large baking dish. Dot with the butter, sprinkle on the sugar and add the rum and lime or lemon juice, more if it seems too sweet.

◆ Dust the bananas with a light grating of nutmeg and bake in a preheated oven for 35 to 40 minutes, until the bananas are tender, brown and aromatic.

◆ Serve hot or warm with plenty of single (light) cream.

◆ OLD-FASHIONED RICE PUDDING ◆

INGREDIENTS

SERVES 6−8

Knob of butter

70 g/2½ oz short-grain (pudding) rice

5 cups/1.2 l/2 pt creamy milk

¼ cup/50 g/2 oz sugar
Vanilla pod OR
¼ cup/50 g/2 oz vanilla sugar (see Spice List)

50 g/2 oz raisins, preferably muscatel

50 g/2 oz almonds, blanched and split

Freshly grated nutmeg

OVEN TEMPERATURE: 150°C/300°F/GAS 2

PREPARATION

◆ Grease an oven-proof dish with the butter and add the rest of the ingredients, except for the nutmeg.
◆ Stir lightly and bake for about 3 hours.
◆ Sprinkle with nutmeg and serve warm, with cream.

◆ BIRTHDAY BREAD-AND-BUTTER PUDDING ◆

INGREDIENTS

SERVES 4

4 thin slices buttered bread, crusts removed, cut in half

50 g/2 oz chopped candied citrus peel

50–75 g/2–3 oz blanched pistachios, halved

50 g/2 oz muscatel raisins, halved

425 ml/15 fl oz single (light) cream

4–5 cardamom pods

25 g/1 oz sugar

3 egg yolks, lightly beaten

OVEN TEMPERATURE: 175°C/350°F/GAS 4

PREPARATION

◆ Layer the bread slices in a greased ovenproof dish with the peel, pistachios and raisins, if used.

◆ Heat the cream with the cardamoms and sugar until almost boiling and pour onto the egg yolks, stirring well.

◆ Strain the mixture over the bread, adding the cardamoms if you would like a stronger flavour.

◆ Set the dish in a roasting pan half-full of hot water and bake until the crust has browned and the custard set, about 30 minutes. Serve warm.

VANILLA BRULEE ◆

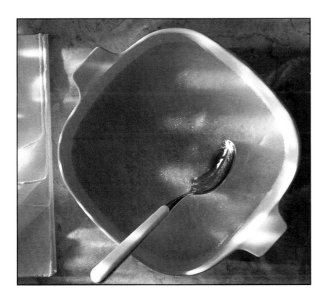

INGREDIENTS

SERVES 4

1 vanilla pod, split and twisted

3 cups/725 ml/1¼ pt double (heavy) or whipping cream

3 egg yolks

½ cup/100 g/4 oz white sugar

½ cup/100 g/4 oz brown sugar

OVEN TEMPERATURE: 150°C/300°F/GAS 2

PREPARATION

◆ Infuse the vanilla pod in the cream over a very low heat (or in a double boiler) for an hour or so, until the cream is well flavoured, then discard the pod. Scrape the seeds into the cream, if you like.

◆ In a double-boiler over barely simmering water whisk the egg yolks and white sugar until thick and pale.

◆ Pour in the cream, whisking all the while, and stir gently until the custard is thick enough to coat the back of a spoon.

◆ Pour the custard into individual ramekins or a shallow gratin dish and put into a roasting tin (pan) half-filled with hot water.

◆ Bake in a preheated oven until a knife comes out just clean, about 1½ hours for a gratin dish, 35 to 45 minutes for ramekins. Chill for at least an hour.

◆ To serve, sprinkle the surface of the custard with an even layer of brown sugar and grill (broil) under a high heat until the sugar caramelizes. Watch it closely, as not too many people like their sugar literally burnt.

◆ PEAR & QUINCE ◆
COMPOTE

INGREDIENTS

SERVES 6

450 g/1 lb cooking pears

450 g/1 lb quinces

½ cup/100 g/4 oz sugar

30 ml/2 tbsp honey

2 cups/450 ml/¾ pt soft red wine

10 g/2 tsp powdered cassia or cinnamon

1 tsp/5 g red sandalwood powder (optional)

30 ml/2 tbsp pear flavoured liqueur (optional)

Pomegranate seeds (optional)

PREPARATION

◆ Peel, quarter and core the fruit, and slice lengthways.

◆ Dissolve the sugar and honey in the wine over a gentle heat until the bottom of the pan no longer feels "gritty" when tapped with a wooden spoon.

◆ Add the fruit, cassia or cinnamon and sandalwood, if used, bring to the boil and simmer, covered, until the fruit is tender, but not mushy. The time depends on how ripe the fruit is.

◆ Carefully lift the fruit slices out of the saucepan and into a serving bowl — a shallow glass one will look pretty.

◆ Bring the cooking liquid to the boil and cook over a high heat for 5 minutes or so, until reduced.

◆ Off the heat, add the liqueur, if used, and taste for sweetness. Either add a little more honey or, if over-sweet, cut with lemon juice. Pour over the pears and quinces, cover and chill.

◆ Serve garnished with pomegranate seeds, if you like, accompanied by a bowl of whipped cream.

◆ BREADS ◆

FLOUR TORTILLAS

INGREDIENTS

MAKES 24

450 g/1 lb plain (all-purpose) flour

10 g/1½ tsp salt

½ cup/100 g/4 oz white vegetable shortening

Approx. 1 cup/225 ml/8 fl oz water

PREPARATION

◆ First of all cut 2 circles, 15 cm (6 in) across, out of thin plastic — a polythene (plastic) bag is ideal.

◆ Sift the flour and salt into a bowl and rub in the shortening.

◆ Add just enough water for the dough to hold together, then knead until it no longer feels sticky.

◆ Divide into 24 pieces and roll each into a ball.

◆ Put a frying-pan (skillet) or a griddle on to heat. No fat is necessary.

◆ Put a dough ball in the centre of one of your plastic circles. Flatten slightly and put the other circle on top. Using these as a guide — and to stop the dough sticking to the work surface and the rolling pin — roll out your tortilla to a roughly circular shape, rotating the rolling pin at each stroke to get an even thickness. Remove the plastic before cooking the tortillas.

◆ Fry each tortilla for about 30 seconds on each side. They should puff slightly and have dark patches.

◆ As they are cooked, wrap them in a tea (dish) towel to keep them warm and supple.

◆ Cooked, they will keep for several days in the fridge, wrapped in their towel and a polythene (plastic) bag, and they also freeze well. To reheat, dry fry for a few moments on each side.

Light and flaky, these dough pancakes from the north of Mexico are far more delicate in flavour than the staple corn tortilla, and considerably easier to make. A very light touch is needed with the rolling pin; Mexican cooks use a short piece of broom handle as they find the conventional rolling pin too heavy. Serve them warm, wrapped around or spread with your choice of topping, or have them for breakfast with butter and jam.

◆ NAN ◆

INGREDIENTS

MAKES 10

25 g/1 oz fresh yeast OR 30 g/1 tbsp dried yeast
15 g/1 tsp sugar
450 g/1 lb plain (all-purpose) flour, warmed
10 g/1½ tsp salt
10 g/1½ tsp baking powder
30 ml/2 tbsp oil
90 ml/6 tbsp natural yogurt
Approx. 1 cup/175 ml/7 fl oz warm water
Garam Masala (bought or see recipe)

OVEN TEMPERATURE: 245°C/475°F/GAS 9

PREPARATION

◆ Cream the yeast and sugar together. Sift the flour, salt and baking powder into a bowl and make a well.

◆ Pour the yeast, oil, yogurt and most of the water and mix well. The mixture should be fairly soft.

◆ Knead the dough until it no longer sticks to your fingers, about 10 minutes.

◆ Put the dough into an oiled polythene (plastic) bag and leave in a warm place until doubled in size. This could take 1½ to 3 hours, depending on the temperature.

◆ Punch down the dough and divide it into 10 pieces. Either roll out on a floured surface or toss from hand to hand — flour them well first — to form an oblong about 6 mm (¼ in) thick.

◆ Sprinkle with garam marsala and bake in a pre-heated oven for about 10 minutes, turning once, until puffed and beginning to brown. Serve warm.

VARIATION Halfway through baking the Nan can be glazed with beaten egg yolk and sprinkled with poppy seeds.

❖ SESAME STICKS ❖

INGREDIENTS

MAKES APPROX. 25
15 g/½ oz fresh yeast OR 5 g/1 tsp dried yeast
5 g/1 tsp sugar
3 cups/350 g/12 oz plain (all-purpose) flour
5 g/1 tsp salt
Pinch of cayenne
5 g/1 tsp ground cumin
1 egg, lightly beaten
4 tbsp/50 g/2 oz butter, melted
Approx. ½ cup/150 ml/¼ pt warm water
50 g/2 oz sesame seeds
OVEN TEMPERATURE: 175°C/350°F/GAS 4

PREPARATION

❖ Cream the yeast and sugar together.

❖ Sift the flour, salt and spices into a warmed bowl and make a well.

❖ Stir in the yeast mixture, egg, melted butter and half the water.

❖ Gradually add enough of the remaining water to form a soft dough.

❖ Knead for about 10 minutes, then put into a clean bowl, cover with a tea (dish) towel and leave to stand in a warm place until doubled in size, which can take up to 2 hours.

❖ Roll golf-ball sized pieces of the dough into sausages about 8 mm (⅓ in) wide and cut into 10-cm (4-in) lengths. Reroll any scraps.

❖ Roll the dough sticks in sesame seeds and arrange them, 2.5 cm (1 in) apart, on ungreased baking trays (cookie sheets).

❖ Bake in a preheated oven for 25 to 30 minutes, until golden brown and crisped through. Serve warm.

VARIATION For Honey Sesame Sticks, use only 2½ g/½ tsp salt, substitute 10 g/2 tsp finely ground aniseed for the cayenne and cumin, and glaze with 45 ml/3 tbsp warmed honey halfway through baking.

❖ BANANA AND GINGER CAKE ❖

INGREDIENTS

1¼ cups/125 g/5 oz plain (all-purpose) flour
10 g/1½–2 tsp ground ginger
2.5 g/½ tsp ground allspice
2.5 g/1½ tsp baking powder
Pinch salt
½ cup/100 g/4 oz soft margarine
½ cup/100 g/4 oz brown sugar
2 eggs
⅔ cup/150 g/6 oz mashed banana (2 medium)
30 g/2 tbsp chopped crystallized ginger or stem ginger in syrup, drained (optional)

ICING

50 g/2 oz icing (confectioners') sugar, well sifted
Approx. 15 ml/1 tbsp lemon juice

OVEN TEMPERATURES: 175°C/350°F/GAS 4, THEN
150°C/300°F/GAS 2

PREPARATION

◆ Sift together the flour, spices, baking powder and salt.

◆ Add the margarine, sugar and eggs and beat until well blended. This is much easier if done in an electric mixer or a food processor.

◆ Lightly stir in the mashed banana and chopped ginger, if used, and turn out into a greased and floured 17.5 × 17.5 cm (7 × 7 in) cake tin (pan).

◆ Bake at 175°C/350°F/Gas 4 for 15 minutes, then reduce the heat to 150°C/300°F/Gas 2 and cook for a further hour or so, until the cake is cooked through. Turn it out onto a wire rack to cool.

◆ For the icing (frosting), gradually add the lemon juice to the icing (confectioners') sugar, stirring well to break down any lumps.

◆ Drizzle the icing (frosting) over the cooled cake and leave to set.

VARIATION For Banana and Ginger Loaf, bake the mixture in a 450-g/1-lb loaf tin (pan) and, instead of icing (frosting) it, serve warm, sliced and buttered.

◆ Hazel Crunch Cookies ◆

INGREDIENTS

MAKES APPROX. 25

½ cup/100 g/4 oz butter or margarine, softened

75 g/3 oz Demerara (light brown) sugar

1 cup/100 g/4 oz plain (all-purpose) flour, or wholemeal if you prefer

*2.5 g/½ tsp mixed spice (or see Sweet Spice Mix)
OR 2½ g/½ tsp ground cardamom*

Good pinch salt

50 g/2 oz rolled oats

75 g/3 oz hazelnuts, toasted and coarsely chopped

Milk or water to mix

OVEN TEMPERATURE: 190°C/375°F/GAS 5

PREPARATION

◆ Cream the butter and sugar together until soft and pale. It helps if you warm the bowl.

◆ Sift in the flour, spice and salt, and add the oats and hazelnuts, plus enough milk or water to hold the mixture together.

◆ Put generous teaspoonfuls on well-greased baking (cookie) sheets, allowing room for them to spread, and flatten slightly with a fork.

◆ Bake in a preheated oven for 12 minutes. Let them cool on their trays for a minute and then remove to a wire rack.

◆ Store in an airtight tin box.

Sweet Saffron Buns

◆ SWEET SAFFRON BUNS ◆

INGREDIENTS

MAKES 12

2.5 g/½ tsp saffron threads

¼ cup/50 ml/2 fl oz hot water

4 cups/450 g/1 lb strong (high gluten) flour, warmed

Good pinch salt

20 g/⅓ oz fresh yeast

⅓ cup/75 g/3 oz sugar

1 cup/225 ml/8 fl oz warm milk

2 tbsp/25 g/1 oz butter, melted

1 egg, beaten

100 g/4 oz chopped candied citrus peel

Egg yolk to glaze

Sugar crystals (optional)

OVEN TEMPERATURE: 220°C/425°F/GAS 7

PREPARATION

◆ Infuse the saffron threads in the hot water for half an hour.

◆ Sift the flour and salt into a warmed bowl and make a well.

◆ Cream the yeast with 5 g/1 tsp of the sugar and add to the warm milk, along with the melted butter, beaten egg and saffron infusion. Stir this lightly into the flour.

◆ Add the remaining sugar and the candied peel and knead to a soft, slightly elastic dough. Leave to rise, covered with a tea (dish) towel, in a warm place for about an hour.

◆ Knead the dough for another minute or two then divide into 12 pieces. Shape into buns and arrange on greased baking (cookie) sheets, allowing room for them to spread.

◆ Leave in a warm place for another half-hour to prove, then bake in a preheated oven for 20 to 25 minutes, glazing with egg yolk, and sprinkling with sugar crystals, if you like, halfway through cooking. The buns are done when the bottoms sound hollow when tapped.

◆ Serve warm, split and buttered. These freeze well.

◆ FRAGRANT FRUIT CAKE ◆

INGREDIENTS

2 cups/225 g/8 oz plain (all-purpose) flour

10–15 g/2–3 tsp mixed spice (bought or see Sweet Spice Mix)

10 g/2 tsp baking powder

Pinch salt

500 g/18 oz mixed dried fruit

225 g/8 oz glacé (candied) cherries, halved

100 g/4 oz cut mixed citrus peel

100 g/4 oz shelled Brazil nuts, halved

125 g/5 oz butter, softened

⅔ cup/150 g/6 oz Demerara (light brown) sugar

4 eggs, lightly beaten

45–60 ml/3-4 tbsp dark rum

15–30 ml/1–2 tbsp milk

75 g/3 oz blanched almonds (optional)

OVEN TEMPERATURES: 175°C/350°F/GAS 4, THEN 150°C/300°F/GAS 2

PREPARATION

◆ Sift the flour with the spice, baking powder and salt into a mixing bowl. Add the fruit, cherries, peel and Brazil nuts and stir until well coated.

◆ Cream the butter and sugar together until pale and fluffy — it helps if you warm the bowl.

◆ Add alternate spoonfuls of the flour and dried fruit mixture, egg, and liquid to the butter and sugar, beating well. If the final mixture seems too stiff add a little more milk.

◆ Turn out into a greased and floured 20 cm (8 in) cake tin (pan) and decorate, if you like, with the almonds.

◆ Wrap a double thickness of brown paper in a collar around the tin, securing it with string, and bake at the higher temperature, in a preheated oven, for half an hour.

◆ Turn down the heat and cook for a further 2 hours or so until a knife or skewer plunged into the centre of the cake comes out clean.

◆ Leave to stand until the tin (pan) is cool enough to touch, then turn the cake out onto a wire rack to cool.

◆ PRESERVES ◆

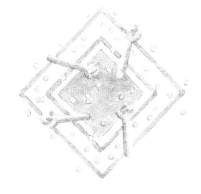

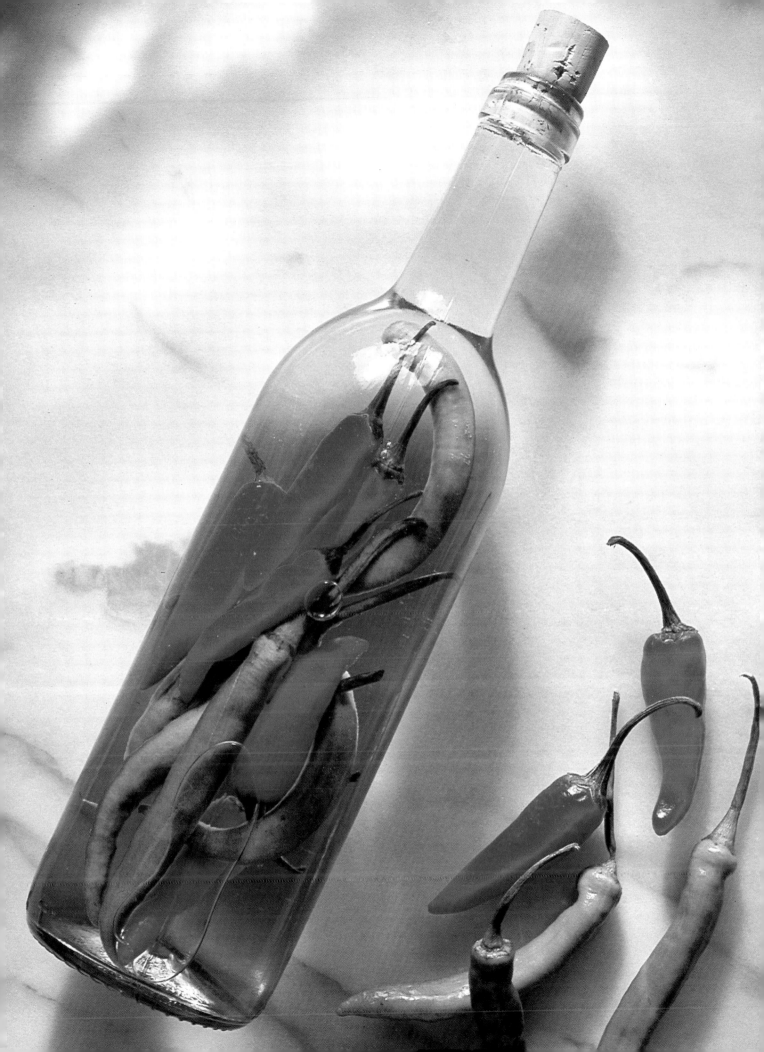

◆ PEPPER WINE ◆

INGREDIENTS

8–12 fresh chillies (chilies), the smaller the better

Dry sherry

PREPARATION

◆ Prick the peppers all over with a needle and put them into a clear glass wine bottle with enough dry sherry to cover them completely.

◆ Stopper tightly with a cork and leave for a week before using. Top up with sherry as the level drops.

VARIATION For a less aesthetic version, the chillies (chilies) can be cut into small pieces. In this case the Pepper Wine will be ready for use in a couple of days.

This old Jamaican recipe not only perks up soups, stews, curries and sauces, but looks beautiful. I keep mine on the kitchen windowsill as an art object. Try to use as much of a colour contrast as possible.

◆ CHILLIES (CHILIES) IN OIL ◆

INGREDIENTS

225 g/8 oz fresh red chillies (chilies), the smaller the better

Olive oil

PREPARATION

◆ Grill (broil) the chillies (chilies) under a high heat until the skins start to blister.

◆ Wrap them in a tea (dish) towel inside a polythene (plastic) bag until cold, then rub off the skins under running water.

◆ Split the chillies (chilies) and gently scrape out the seeds. Rinse well. Put them into small jars and pour over enough olive oil just to cover them. Screw on the lids and leave for 2 to 3 weeks before using, so that the flavour can develop.

❖ WINDFALL CHUTNEY ❖

INGREDIENTS

MAKES APPROX. 2 KG / 4 ½ LB

8 dried red chillies (chilies)

1.4 kg/3 lb windfall apples and pears, mixed, peeled, cored and finely chopped

2 medium onions, finely chopped

225 g/8 oz sultanas (golden raisins)

350 g/12 oz soft brown sugar

10 g/2 tsp salt

10 g/2 tsp ground allspice

2½ cups/600 ml/1 pt malt vinegar

PREPARATION

❖ Soak the dried chillies (chilies) in hot water for half an hour, then chop finely. Put the chillies into a large preserving pan with the rest of the ingredients and gradually add the vinegar, stirring from time to time, until all the vinegar is absorbed. This should take about an hour.

❖ Pot in warmed jars, covering the surface with circles of greaseproof (waxed) paper. Seal, label and leave to mature for a month before using.

Instant Ginger Relish

◆ Instant Ginger Relish ◆

INGREDIENTS

MAKES APPROX. 1¼ CUPS / 300 ML / ½ PT
225 g/8 oz fresh root ginger
5 g/1 tsp salt
10 g/2 tsp sugar
Juice of 2 limes
A little dry sherry

PREPARATION

◆ Peel and coarsely grate the ginger. Sprinkle it with the salt and leave to stand for 10 minutes.

◆ Rinse the ginger under running water and squeeze out excess liquid. Put into a small bowl with the sugar and lime juice and mix well.

◆ Pack the relish into a small, screw-top jar (or jars) and top up with enough dry sherry to cover the ginger. Cover tightly and store in the fridge.

The fresh taste of this relish goes well with most cold meats, especially pork and ham, and is a flavourful addition to mixed salads.

◆ Peach Pickle ◆

INGREDIENTS

MAKES APPROX. 1½ KG / 3¼ LB
15 g/1 tbsp tamarind, pulp or dried
60 ml/4 tbsp hot water
2½ cups/600 ml/1 pt white wine vinegar
5 cm/2 in fresh ginger, peeled and grated
15 g/1 tbsp ground coriander
1¼ cups/300 g/10 oz sugar
5 g/1 tsp cayenne
Good pinch salt
Generous 1 kg/2 lb ripe peaches

PREPARATION

◆ Soak the tamarind in the hot water for half an hour. Squeeze out and reserve the liquid.

◆ Combine the rest of the ingredients, except for the peaches, in a mixing bowl and add the tamarind water.

◆ Loosen the peach skins by pouring boiling water over them and then refreshing with cold. Slip off the skins, halve the peaches, remove the stones (pits) and slice or cube the flesh into a heavy sauce-pan.

◆ Add the vinegar mixture and bring to the boil. Simmer for 8 to 10 minutes, pour into sterilized, warmed jars and leave to cool.

◆ Cover, seal and refrigerate for a week before using. Once opened, keep the pickle in the fridge.

◆ SWEET SPICE MIX ◆

INGREDIENTS

4 parts allspice
2 parts coriander
1 part stick cinnamon, broken
1 part 5-spice
1 part nutmeg
1 part dried ginger
1 part caraway

PREPARATION

◆ Heat the spices in a moderate oven until fragrant, then grind them together in a spice grinder or coffee grinder.

◆ Sift and store in an opaque, airtight container.

VARIATION Cumin, star anise and cardamom seeds (discard the pods) can also be incorporated into the mixture.

Home-made mixed spice is so much nicer than bought for cakes and baking — far more aromatic and not so reliant on the cheaper and more easily available spices, such as the ubiquitous cinnamon. The blend suggested below I find equally good in fruit cakes, pastries, biscuits (cookies) and with cooked fruit, especially stewed apples or pears, though of course you can adapt the proportions to suit yourself. It is also excellent as pumpkin pie spice.

◆ CURRY PASTE ◆

INGREDIENTS

8 parts coriander seed

2 parts cumin seed

3 parts turmeric

2 parts fenugreek

1 part mustard seed

1 part black pepper

2 parts dried red chillies (chilies), soaked in hot water for half an hour, then finely ground

1 part garlic, crushed (minced)

1 part peeled root ginger, finely minced

A little vinegar

Oil for frying, preferably mustard oil

PREPARATION

➤ Warm the first 6 ingredients through in a moderate oven to release the aromas, then grind them finely in a spice grinder or coffee grinder. Add enough vinegar to make a paste.

➤ Heat some oil in a well-dried frying pan and stir the chillies (chilies), garlic and ginger for a minute or so without browning.

➤ Add the spice mixture and fry until thick and smooth.

➤ Cool and store in an opaque, airtight container.

➤ 15 ml/1 tbsp should be enough to flavour a curry for 4 people.

If you make a lot of curries, or mind what goes into them, or simply fancy a shortcut, it is worth having your own blend of curry paste handy, using the ingredients and proportions listed below as a guide.

◆ GARAM MASALA ◆

INGREDIENTS

4 parts coriander seed
2 parts black peppercorns
2 parts caraway seed
1 part cardamom seeds (i.e. husks removed)
1 part cumin seeds
1 part cloves
1 part stick cinnamon, broken
1 part nutmeg, freshly grated
1 part mace blades

PREPARATION

◆ Warm the spices through in a moderate oven to release the aromas, then grind in a spice or coffee grinder and sift them.

◆ Store in an opaque, airtight container. This should keep its flavour for up to 3 weeks.

One of the joys of this fragrant lynchpin of Asian cuisine is the lack of any set recipe, so why not follow their cooks' example and create your own blend.

◆ INDEX ◆